About the Book

Since the days of prehistory, man has been devising weapons for defense and attack. Old arms were discarded when newer, more effective weapons were developed—often against the outraged cries of traditionalists. Years after the medieval knights adopted the bow, once labeled the coward's weapon, they warned that the use of guns would mean the death of chivalry and bravery in battle.

As Peter Limburg's well-informed essays trace the word derivations for each weapon, he provides the reader with many useful and fascinating historical anecdotes and insights, as he also shows how each weapon was used, why it was valued, and why it came to be replaced. Readers with many diverse interests will appreciate Mr. Limburg's rewarding text, which is augmented by W. K. Plummer's carefully researched illustrations.

WHAT'S IN THE NAMES OF
ANTIQUE WEAPONS

by Peter Limburg

Illustrated by W. K. Plummer

COWARD, McCANN & GEOGHEGAN, INC. • NEW YORK

A What's-Behind-the-Word Book

SBN: GB-698-30485-3

SBN: TR-698-20233-3

Library of Congress Catalog Card Number: 72-85619
PRINTED IN THE UNITED STATES OF AMERICA

*To my fellow sufferers in
"The Late Company B," 364th Inf. Regt.,
and everyone else who had to
learn the difference between
a "rifle" and a "gun"
the hard way*

𝕮eapon comes

from the Anglo-Saxon word *waepen*, meaning an instrument used in war, combat, or hunting. It has been traced back to an old Germanic root, *waepnom*, and it has close relatives in some present-day languages, such as Swedish *vapen*, Dutch *wapen*, and German *Waffe*. (The *Luftwaffe*, the dreaded German air force of World War II, was literally the "air weapon.")

Weapons and tools have a common ancestry, and many ordinary tools can be used as weapons. For instance, a screwdriver can be a lethal stabbing weapon. A plumber's wrench can crush a person's skull. A pick handle makes a highly effective club. It would not be inaccurate to say that weapons are specialized tools designed for killing or disabling.

7

However, weapons cannot be used to perform the jobs of ordinary tools. They are not designed for it, and they are not meant to be used that way. You could try to pry open a crate with a sword, but you would probably bend or snap the blade. A crowbar would do the job faster and better.

This book deals with antique weapons. *Antique* comes from the Latin *antiquus*, meaning "old." Just how old an object has to be to qualify as an antique is an arguable question. To a second-hand dealer, a fifty-year-old table might be an "antique." To a museum curator, the same table might be "a piece of old junk."

Weapons experts, museums, and collectors generally agree that the cutoff date for "antique weapons" is about the end of the American Civil War (1865). Of course, many weapons that were first made centuries ago are also used in modern times— for example, the pistol and the rifle, not to mention the hand grenade. Daggers go back to the flint knife of the Stone Age hunter, but they are used right now by commandos. They are discussed here because of their antique origins.

This book is divided into two parts. The first part covers weapons that are not firearms; the second deals with firearms.

There is not room here for all the weapons that might qualify for inclusion, and some have unavoidably been left out. For instance, revolver-type guns were being made before 1600 (although they never worked right), and a workable revolver was patented by a Boston man named Elisha Collier in 1819. But revolvers are not covered here, in part because they are not generally considered antique weapons.

Weapon has acquired many additional meanings. One of these is "anything that serves for attack or defense." A philosopher has said that one of the best weapons is silence. And here I rest my case.

Part 1

Armor comes

from the Old French word *armeure* or *armure*, which is derived from the Latin word *armatura*. Language scholars have traced it back to an ancient Indo-European root, *ar-*, meaning "to fit or join things together." If you examine a suit of armor, you will see that it is indeed made up of parts that are fitted and joined together. In fact, it would not work otherwise. *Armatura* could mean either "armor" or "weapons," and the English word *armor*, which dates from the 1200's, originally had both meanings.

When we think of armor, the first thing that comes to most people's minds is a medieval knight covered with steel plates from head to toe. But this was the high point of many centuries of development. No one knows just how old an invention armor is, but the earliest civilizations have left pictures and statues of men wearing armor. Some of these are nearly five thousand years old.

The earliest armor was probably not made of metal, for metal was scarce and expensive in ancient times. One material that was used very early for armor was leather. When leather is soaked in hot water, it can be shaped and molded easily. When it dries out, it becomes stiff and hard, like the sole of a shoe. It makes an effective armor, though not as durable as metal. Leather armor was still being used as late as the mid-1600's.

For centuries after metal armor came into use, it was used only to protect the most vulnerable parts of the body. The Greeks of classical times, for instance, wore a bronze breastplate, bronze shin guards, and a sort of metal belly protector—at least those who could afford metal armor did so.

Others wore armor of leather or quilted cloth. Actually, quilted armor is surprisingly hard to pierce with sword or spear, and it absorbs the shock of a blow well. It is made by stuffing rags or other soft material between two layers of strong cloth and then quilting it—that is, stitching the cloth into little squares or diamonds to keep the stuffing in place. Cloth armor can also be made by stitching together a number of layers of cloth without stuffing. Either way, it is more comfortable than metal armor.

The Romans wore armor much like that of the Greeks, except that their shoulders and backs, as well as their chests, were protected. This armored top, plus shin guards and a shield, was all the protection a Roman legionary was supposed to need. Adding more armor would have made it more difficult for the Roman soldiers to march and would have interfered with their freedom of movement in battle.

By the time the Normans invaded England, A.D. 1066, a different type of armor was generally used. This was mail, sometimes called *chain mail*. Mail was made of hundreds of tiny rings of iron or steel, linked together to form a metal mesh. Mail had the great advantage of being completely flexible, and it was fairly effective in stopping a sword or spear. But it had no cushioning power, so that a man wearing mail could be disabled by the force of a blow even if it did not draw blood.

12

Mail may have been invented by the Persians. By the second century B.C. the Romans had begun to use it for some of their soldiers, and its use spread gradually to other European peoples. The Romans called mail *macula*, meaning both "spot" and "mesh of a net." In French, this became *maille*. After the Norman conquest of England, *maille* became part of the English language.

At the Battle of Hastings, where England's fate was decided, both Normans and Saxons wore a kind of long shirt of mail, which the Normans called a *hawberk* and the Saxons called a *byrnie*.

Hawberk comes from two old Germanic roots, *Hals*, meaning "neck," and *bergan*, meaning "to protect." Literally, it meant "neck protector." *Byrnie* goes back to another Germanic root, *brynjon*, which may be derived from a Celtic word referring to the chest.

The hawberk hung down to the wearer's knee; it was slit up to the crotch so that he could move his legs. It was usually made with an attached hood of mail to protect the head. Some warriors wore a helmet over the hood for extra protection.

In the 1100's, knights and professional soldiers began wearing a quilted jacket under their coats of mail to cushion blows and to keep from being chafed by the metal garment. This jacket was called an *aketon* or *haketon*, from the Arabic *al-qutun*, meaning "cotton," the material with which it was usually stuffed.

By the early 1200's the age of chivalry was well under way, and knights did a great deal of fighting with lances, especially in tournaments. They needed armor that could ward off a sharp-pointed lance with the weight of a man and a charging horse behind it. Mail could not do this, so plate armor came into being.

Plate armor was made of thin steel plates, tempered to make them hard and springy, so that a lance or sword would glance off. The breastplate was the first piece of plate armor to be used. Then came thigh guards. Bit by bit, other pieces were added to protect the knight's knees, shoulders, arms, hands, and feet. By the 1400's a fully equipped knight was covered by steel plates from head to toe, except for the seat of his pants, which was not exposed when he was sitting on his horse. Not every knight could afford a full suit of plate armor, and poor knights had to get along without the less essential pieces.

A suit of plate armor was composed of a number of subassemblies. Each subassembly—breast and back plates, arm guards, thigh guards, shin guards, and the rest—was buckled on separately and laced together by the knight's squire. Where joints

HORSE ARMOR
MILAN, C. 1450

were needed, as in the fingers of the gloves or the elbows of the arm guards, the plates were loosely riveted together, hinge-fashion. For security they were also riveted to leather straps inside the armor.

A full suit of armor weighed from 50 to 75 pounds. This was quite a load to carry around, but the weight was well distributed, and a knight in good condition could fight perfectly well on foot and mount his horse without help. However, a fully armored knight sometimes collapsed from heat prostration, for in the sun the armor became like an oven. Heart attacks from the violent exertion of combat under the extra load of metal were not unknown either.

Common soldiers did not have this problem. They usually fought in leather or quilted armor, unless they were lucky enough to take a mail shirt or a breast plate from a dead or badly wounded enemy. Soldiers were also known to strip the corpses of their friends after a battle. In the later Middle Ages, however, some rulers began to equip their soldiers with partial armor.

As armor improved, so did the weapons used against it. At close range, a crossbow bolt or a longbow arrow could penetrate even plate armor with a square hit, and a number of weapons such as the poleax and the halberd were expressly designed to punch holes in armor or pry it apart at the joints. But it was gunpowder that actually spelled the doom of armor. It was no trick for armorers to make armor that could withstand the heaviest musket ball. The trouble was that such armor was much too heavy for anyone to wear. Soldiers began to discard their armor bit by bit, preferring to take their chances rather than lug all that weight around. The knights followed suit. By 1700 armor was as out of date as last year's automobile models are today.

A whole dictionary could be written about armor alone—its varying types and styles and the pieces of which it was made up. Here are a few armor terms that have not been covered above:

Brigandine was a chest and back protector made of small plates of steel or horn riveted to the inside of a quilted, sleeveless jacket. The brigandine, introduced in the 1400's, was worn by foot soldiers and archers. Its name comes from *brigand*, a fourteenth-century French word that originally meant a lightly armored part-time soldier. By the fifteenth century *brigand* had come to mean a bandit or highway robber, which tells us something about the way soldiers were apt to behave in those days.

A cheaper version of the brigandine was the *jack*, which had its plates tied to the cloth instead of riveted on. The name is an English adaptation of a French term, *jaque*, whose origin is un-

SKULL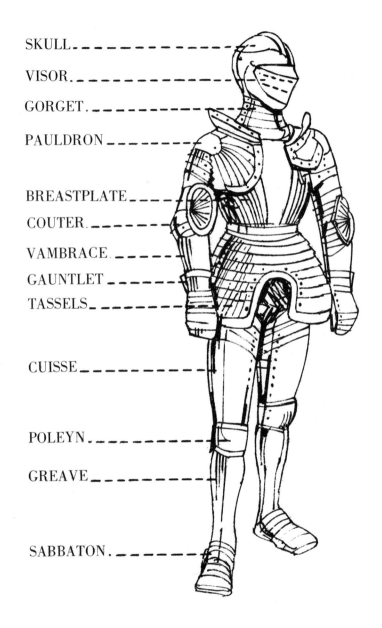

VISOR

GORGET

PAULDRON

BREASTPLATE

COUTER

VAMBRACE

GAUNTLET

TASSELS

CUISSE

POLEYN

GREAVE

SABBATON

known. Our modern word *jacket* is a diminutive form of the old foot soldier's jack.

Cuirass was a breastplate and backplate combination or sometimes the breastplate alone. Usually made of metal, it was originally made of leather, and its name comes from the French word for "leather," *cuir*.

Greave was a metal shin guard. In the Middle Ages it was improved by adding a rear half to protect the calf of the leg. The two halves were hinged along one side and fastened by buckles on the other side. *Greave* (usually used in the plural form, *greaves*) comes from *grève*, an Old French word for the shin.

Gauntlet was an armored glove made of plates of steel sewed onto leather. The fingers could bend and unbend freely, which was vital for gripping a weapon. For tournaments there were special gauntlets with fingers that locked in position automatically when the knight took a grip on his lance. This made it almost impossible for the knight to drop his lance when he hit his opponent. The gauntlet's fingers were released afterward by the knight's squire.

Knights who were proud of their fighting prowess were constantly looking for other knights to challenge. A popular form of challenge was to fling your gauntlet crashing down at the feet of the challengee. He would accept by picking it up. From this custom come the expressions "flinging down the gauntlet" and "taking up the gauntlet."

Gauntlet comes from the French *gant* ("glove"), which is derived from *want*, a West German word meaning "mitten." The *-let* is a diminutive ending that was not actually used in English until the age of chivalry was pretty well over. It is hard to see how the huge, armored glove of a knight could be called a *little glove*, but almost anything is possible where words and their meanings are concerned. *See also* HELMET; SHIELD.

Arms in

the sense of weapons, comes from the Latin word *arma*, of the same meaning. *Arma* was one of a small group of Latin words that existed only in the plural; they had no singular form. In the case of *arms*, English follows this old and illogical Latin rule. Very seldom do you hear anyone speak of "an arm" or see the word in print. *Arms* came into English by way of the French word *armes*, which was introduced by the Normans. The native Anglo-Saxon word was *waepen*, from which *weapon* comes.

Arms may be classified in any number of ways. They may be offensive (swords, bows, rifles) or defensive (helmets, shields, armor). They may be weapons for hand-to-hand fighting (again like the sword) or used at a distance (crossbow, javelin, gun). *Small arms* refers to all weapons that are carried and used by one person. This includes swords, spears, battle-axes, pistols, rifles, and so on. *Sidearms* refers to weapons such as pistols, daggers, and bayonets, which are worn at the side when not in use. *Shoulder arms* are those which are held at the user's shoulder— for example, rifles, muskets, and carbines. These last three are all FIREARMS, which is covered in a separate entry.

Arms has another meaning quite separate from that of weapons. This is the *heraldic arms,* or symbols belonging to aristocratic families. Heraldic arms originated around the mid-1100's, when knights began painting symbols on their shields to identify themselves to friend and foe. Sometimes these symbols were geometrical patterns, such as stripes, checkers, and crosses. Sometimes they were a play on the name of the knight's family. For instance, an English knight named Applegarth used three apples for his symbol, and another named Horseley used a horse's head.

About this time, too, knights began to wear a long, sleeveless coat over their armor, which some called a *surcoat* (literally, "over-coat") and others called a *coat of arms* because it went over the armor. The French invented both terms, as they did most of the terms of chivalry. *Coat of arms* is simply an English translation of the medieval French term *cotte d'armes.*

It became fashionable for knights to wear their heraldic symbols on their coats, as well as on their shields, and so *coat of arms* came to mean the symbols themselves. Later, *arms* came to carry this meaning by itself, so that we speak of the arms of the Tudors, the arms of the Hapsburgs, and so on.

That medieval French word *cotte,* which gave us *coat of arms* also gave us the ordinary *coat.* It was derived from a late Latin word, *cotta,* which originally meant a kind of coarse woolen cloth and later a cloak made of that material.

Arrow comes

from an old Germanic word, *arhwon*, meaning "something be-longing to the bow." *Arhw* was the old Germanic word for "bow," and it is related to the Latin word for "bow," *arcus*.

The first arrows were probably pointed sticks whose ends had been hardened in a fire. (Some primitive peoples were still using arrows like this not very many years ago.) But men learned thousands of years ago to make points of sharpened stone or bone. Many types of arrowheads were developed: small, light ones for shooting small animals; big, heavy arrowheads with more penetrating power for shooting big animals; blunt ones for knocking down birds without tearing up their flesh; forked-prong arrowheads for shooting fish; and, for warfare, barbed arrowheads that the enemy could not pull out without making the wound much worse. These patterns were copied when men learned to make arrowheads of metal, about 5000 B.C.

An arrow had to be straight and evenly balanced in order to fly straight. A crooked or unbalanced arrow would go wide of the target. Feathers, usually three in number, were glued to the tail end of the arrow. The feathers acted like stabilizer fins and helped keep the arrow on course.

Arrows were usually carried in a holder called a *quiver*. This term comes from an Old French word, *quivre* or *coivre*, which was brought to England by the Normans. Sometime before 1500, it became *quiver*, although before English spelling was standardized, it had some strange variations, such as *quyuer*.

The verb *to quiver*, in the sense of trembling or shaking, comes from an entirely different source, the medieval English word *cwafien*, which also gave us *quaver*.

For people of the ancient world, arrows had all kinds of magical significance. Primitive tribesmen used to shoot arrows at the sky to stop an eclipse of the sun or to bring rain. The Greeks and Romans believed that falling in love was caused by the god Eros (Cupid) shooting people with his enchanted arrows. (Ancient peoples thought that romantic love was a kind of mental sickness, if not a downright calamity, so they blamed it on a god.)

The arrow has always been a symbol of swiftness. "Swift as an arrow" used to be a popular expression, although nowadays the bullet has replaced the arrow to some extent as a symbol of speed.

Assegai was

a spear that conquered an empire in the south of Africa. It was invented around 1810 by a young Zulu warrior named Chaka.

At the time, Chaka was serving in the army of the Mtetwa tribe. His own tribe, the Zulus, had treated Chaka and his mother cruelly because he had been born out of wedlock. They found refuge with the Mtetwas, a related tribe, who treated them kindly. Chaka became the champion fighter of the Mtetwas, representing them against rival tribes.

The Mtetwas, the Zulus, and related tribes of southeastern Africa fought their battles according to a strict and formal ritual. A champion from each tribe would step forward, and the two men would exchange taunts. They they would hurl javelins at each other from a distance of 50 yards. Each fighter would dodge the other man's spears, pick them up, and throw them back until one of them was wounded or exhausted or lost his nerve and fled. Then the winning side would take a few prisoners, and the losers would ransom them with cattle.

Chaka would have none of this. A hard, embittered man, he was out for blood. He had had a specially broad and heavy spearhead made by a blacksmith, and he had fitted it to a heavy 4-foot shaft. This spear was useless for throwing, but it made an ideal stabbing weapon for hand-to-hand fighting. The smith who had forged the spearhead had a sinister reputation as a sorcerer, and Chaka was delighted to let his friends think that his new weapon was bewitched.

When he was called upon to fight as the champion of his adopted tribe, Chaka took the spear he had designed. Coldly and contemptuously he stood his ground while the other tribe jeered at him and his ridiculous weapon. Then he trotted slowly forward, dodging the opposing champion's allotted three javelins and disdaining to pick them up. While the astounded spectators wondered what in the world was going on, Chaka charged the helpless warrior and stabbed him through the heart. Chaka's companions then attacked the members of the other tribe, killing them without mercy.

Chaka soon became a renowned military leader and a man of great wealth. Then he seized the throne of his own people, the Zulus. His highly disciplined, assegai-armed fighters marched onward, conquering tribe after tribe, until Chaka ruled an area about as big as Colorado and Wyoming together. His successors conquered still more territory for the Zulu empire.

Although the Zulus made it famous, the assegai's name did not come from Zulu or from any other sub-Saharan language. It was originally an Arab word, *az-zaghayah*, which was the name of a light spear used by Berber tribesmen of North Africa. Portuguese and French traders who did business with the North African Arabs picked up this word, changing it to *azagaya* or *azagaye* to fit their own pronunciations better.

In the late 1800's, European colonists in South Africa were fighting full-scale wars against Zulus who wanted to colonize the same area. The newspapers picked up the name "assegai," which after all was "African," even though it came from the other end of the continent and referred to a different kind of spear, and they used it in their colorful reports of the battles between white and black. Thus did the Arab name, misspelled, come to be given to the Zulu weapon.

Battle-ax was

a type of ax designed for use in combat. Knights of the Middle Ages carried battle-axes along with their lances and swords.

The medieval battle-ax had a chunky, wedge-shaped head on the end of a 3- or 4-foot handle. Its narrow cutting edge could punch through steel armor. The handle often ended in a metal spearpoint, so that the ax could be used for stabbing, as well as chopping.

A knight armed with a battle-ax could deal his opponent a disabling wound or, if he were strong enough, cleave right through his helmet and split his skull. However, the knights preferred not to kill each other if they could avoid it. A captured knight could be held for a big ransom, but a dead one could not. In addition, no matter how much two knights might dislike each other, they were bound together by a sort of group loyalty.

Battle-axes have been used in one form or another ever since prehistoric men learned how to shape a stone and fasten it to the end of a stick. The tomahawk of the North American Indians was a primitive type of battle-ax. In Mexico, the Aztecs had a kind of battle-ax of heavy wood edged with razor-sharp flakes of obsidian rock.

The ancient civilization of Crete, which flourished 3,000 years before the Christian Era, worshiped a curious sort of double-headed ax called a *labrys*. This may originally have been a battle-ax used by the ancestors of the Cretans. The famous labyrinth of mythology was actually the great palace of Crete's rulers at Knossos. Its name meant "house of the double-headed ax."

Battle-ax is also a slang term for a disagreeable, aggressive woman, usually middle-aged or elderly. This term needs no explanation.

The word *ax* comes from the Anglo-Saxon word *aex*. It is related to the Greek word *axine*, which once meant an ax but now means a "mattock" or "pick" (both digging tools). The meaning of the Greek word changed, but the idea of chopping is still there.

Battle entered the English language as the Old French word *batayle*, probably not long after the Norman conquest of England. It had taken on its modern spelling by the eighteenth century. Language scholars trace *battle* back to a rare Latin word, *battuere*, which referred to pounding meat to tenderize it before cooking—not a bad description of what happened in an old-time battle.

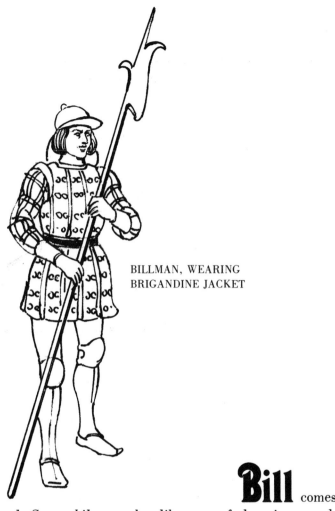

BILLMAN, WEARING
BRIGANDINE JACKET

Bill comes
from the Anglo-Saxon *bil*, a machetelike type of chopping sword.
The name may be derived from an Indo-European root meaning
"to cleave."

Knights did not use the bill. It was a peasant's and foot soldier's weapon. The bill was developed from the old-time peasant's pruning hook, which had a broad, long, heavy blade that
curved around into a hook at one end. Like a modern brush
hook, it was used for clearing away bushes and trimming

branches from trees. In warfare, the blade could chop a good-sized wound into an opponent, while the hook could be used to drag a knight from his relatively safe perch on horseback. The bill was mounted on a strong pole 6 feet or so in length.

The bill was a very old weapon. In England, at least, it was being used before 1066, and it was probably used by farmers all over northern Europe. In the 1300's it was given an armor-piercing spike on the back of the blade, plus a spearpoint jutting out from the end of the pole. More elaborate versions were also made.

In the 1400's the bill was very popular among Englishmen, and it was romanticized in folktales and ballads, much as the Colt .45 is romanticized in stories of the American West. It was fondly called the *brown bill*, perhaps because the process of tempering its metal gave it a brown color.

The bill passed out of military use in the 1500's, as men gradually gave up wearing body armor, but watchmen and constables were armed with bills until the end of the 1600's.

The bill that you get from a store comes from a different source, the medieval English word *bille*. This was an Anglicized version of the Latin *bulla*, meaning "seal." People also used *bulla* to mean a "sealed document," and *bulla* and *bille* came to be used for all kinds of legal papers. Later *bill* took on the meaning of an itemized list, as in the phrase "Bill of Rights." The particular meaning of a list of things for which money is owed goes back as far as the 1400's.

Bow comes
from an old Germanic root, *bug-*, that carries the meaning of
"bending." It is bending—and straightening out again when released—that gives the bow its force. A physicist might say that
a bow is a mechanism for storing energy. When you hold the bow
in one hand and draw back the string with your other hand, bending
the bow into a curve, you are putting energy into it. When you let
go, this energy is released, and the bow snaps back to its original

29

shape, pulling the string straight with enough force to send an arrow flying for many feet.

The Old English word for "bow" was *boga*. By the fourteenth century, when Chaucer wrote his *Canterbury Tales*, the *g* had dropped out, and people said *bowe*, with the *e* pronounced something like the *a* in sofa. Later the *e* disappeared from speech and writing, leaving the modern word *bow*.

The Latin word for "bow" was *arcus*. In French, this became *arc*, while the man who used the bow was called an *archier*. In English, this became *archer*. *Archery*, the art of shooting with a bow and arrow, comes from the related Old French word *archerie*.

The Greek word for "bow" was *toxon*, from which a number of pompous and high-flown words dealing with archery have been derived. One such word is *toxophilite*, or "bow lover." An archery club called the Royal Toxophilite Society was founded in England in 1781.

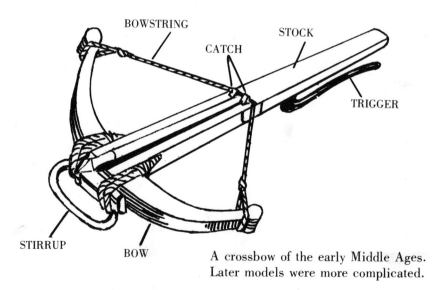

A crossbow of the early Middle Ages. Later models were more complicated.

Our word *toxic*, meaning "poisonous," is also derived from the Greek word for "bow." It was originally *toxikon pharmakon*, or "bow poison"—that is, poison for smearing on arrows. *Pharmakon* meant both "poison" and "medicine" to the ancient Greeks. Perhaps they didn't think there was much difference between the two.

The bow is a very old invention. Cave paintings more than 15,000 years old show men using bows to shoot animals. Soon enough, men discovered that the bow was as useful in war as it was in hunting. However, warriors of certain peoples refused to use the bow because they thought it was a coward's weapon: You could wound or kill an opponent without coming close enough for him to reach you with his club or spear.

This attitude lasted for thousands of years. Knights of the Middle Ages shared this traditional contempt for the bowman—which did not prevent them from falling victim to a well-placed arrow.

There are three major types of bow: the *short bow*, the *longbow*, and the *crossbow*. Early bows were mostly short, 3 to 4 feet long. The famous English longbow came on the scene relatively late. It was a twelfth-century invention, originating in Wales. The longbow was supposed to be as tall as its user, and in those days the average height of a grown man was about five feet. Longbows of six feet or even more were not uncommon, though.

The bigger the bow, the more strength it took to pull it. Some people, to make an impression, would sport a bow that was too big for them to handle. This form of boasting was called *overbowing*. However, a person engaging in this form of bragging was careful to find an excuse for not actually shooting his bow—for obvious reasons.

The longbow shot an arrow $2\frac{1}{2}$ to 3 feet in length. In the hands of a well-trained archer, it had an effective range of some 200 yards and a maximum range of 300 to 350 yards, depending on the size of the bow and the strength of the archer. At close range, it could pierce plate armor.

Before the longbow was perfected, the deadliest shooting weapon on the battlefield was the crossbow. (For details, see the separate entry on CROSSBOW.) The crossbow was accurate and powerful. Almost anyone could handle it with little training. But it was slow, because it took a long time to get it ready to shoot. The longbow had greater range and a much faster rate of fire than the crossbow. After a series of decisive victories in the fourteenth century, the longbow began to push the crossbow off the battlefield.

But the longbow, too, had its drawbacks. It was a marvelously effective weapon in the hands of a good bowman. But it took above-average strength, skill, and years of training to handle it properly. You could not take a man from behind the plow and turn him into a bowman in a week, a month, or even a year.

In time, therefore, the longbow was replaced by the gun, which required little strength and less skill on the part of its user. England, for example, did away with bows in the regular army in 1595. No longer needed for military purposes, the bow soon fell out of favor with civilians as well.

In the late eighteenth century there was a romantic revival of interest in things of the past, including archery. The revival of archery as a sport dates from this period. Today it still has a devoted, though limited, following.

When a sports announcer says that the coach is sending in the "second string," he is using an expression derived from archery. Bowmen made a habit of carrying a spare bowstring in case of an emergency. If the first string broke in the midst of a battle, the bowman could quickly replace it with his second string.

ONAGER

Catapult is

a general name for the ancient siege engines that hurled rocks and other missiles at the walls of castles and cities. The first catapult was invented shortly after 400 B.C. Dionysius, the dictator of the Greek colony of Syracuse, in Sicily, had hired a number of ingenious craftsmen to create new and terrible weapons for him to use in attacking rival colonies. His corps of experts came up with a giant bow set crosswise on a pedestal. To this they gave the name *katapeltes*, from the Greek *kata* ("down" or "against") and *pallein* ("to hurl").

Behind the bow of the catapult stretched a wooden trough with a movable slide resting in it. The catapult crew pushed the slide forward and hooked it onto the bowstring. Then they pulled it back with the aid of a windlass, bending the bow. A system of catches held the slide in place. Then the crew laid a giant dart, up to 6 feet long, in a groove on the top of the slide, just ahead of the bowstring. When the order to shoot was given, one of the crew yanked a cord attached to a trigger, the bowstring twanged forward, and the missile was on its way.

At first catapults were regarded—by those who did not possess them—as a violation of the code of honorable warfare. But soon catapults were being used throughout the Mediterranean area. The Romans learned about the catapult from the Greeks, but they changed the Greek name to *catapulta* to make it sound more like a native Latin word.

Very large catapults were built for hurling stone balls weighing as much as 180 pounds. A small, portable, one-man catapult was also invented. This was the *gastraphetes* (Greek for "belly weapon"), which was the first crossbow. The effective range of the heavy stone throwers was somewhat over 100 yards, while the dart throwers were effective up to 600 yards and occasionally farther.

Another development was the use of *torsion* power (from the Latin *torquere*, "to twist"). Instead of a bow, a torsion catapult had a frame with a thick, tightly twisted skein of hair at each end. A short wooden arm was stuck into the center of each skein; the free ends of the arms were connected to the bowstring. When the string was drawn back, it pulled back on the arms and made them twist the skeins even tighter, storing up power the way a twisted rubber band does. The skeins were more powerful than a bow, but a torsion catapult got out of order more frequently than one of the bow type, and so both types were used together.

The Romans gave the catapult a second name, *ballista*, which comes from the Greek word *ballein*, "to toss or throw." (The

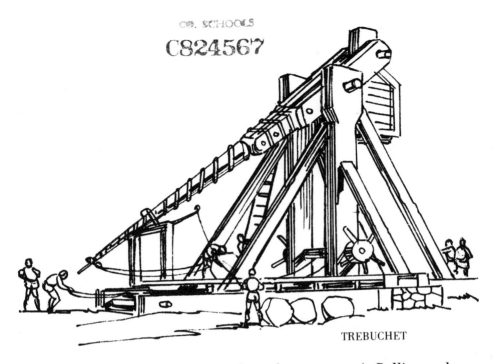

TREBUCHET

modern word *ballistics* comes from the same root.) *Ballista* and *catapulta* thus both meant "thrower," and the two words were used pretty much interchangeably.

In the early Christian Era a new type of siege engine came into use. This was the *onager*, named for a wild ass of the Near East that was said to kick stones at its enemies. The onager had a long wooden throwing arm that ended in a giant spoon. It was powered by a very large skein of twisted cordage. The crew, heaving on wooden bars, wound up the skein until it brought the throwing arm up against a padded crossbeam. The skein and its winding bars were then locked in place, and the crew hauled the arm down with a windlass, making the skein tighter yet. The arm was tied down with a strong rope, and the crew loaded a heavy stone or ball of metal in the spoon. When the rope was released, the arm flew up and struck the padded crossbeam, and the missile

35

went hurtling off through the air toward its target. The onager was used well into the Middle Ages; in medieval times it was called the *mangonel*, from the Greek *manganon*, meaning "mechanical contrivance."

The last kind of catapult to be developed was the *trebuchet*, which was invented in the twelfth century A.D. It was the largest of the catapult devices. The trebuchet, whose name comes from an Old French word meaning "to overturn," was a tall, massive framework on top of which a long pole was pivoted like a seesaw. The pivot was placed so that the pole had a long arm and a short arm. The long arm was fitted with a sling for holding missiles. The short arm held a heavy counterweight, usually a big box filled with stones. The long arm was pulled down and loaded, as with the onager. When it was released, the counterweight flipped the long arm up with tremendous force. A big trebuchet could throw a 200-pound stone high in the air and over the wall of a castle.

Club comes
from the Middle English word *clubbe*, which in turn comes from
the Old Norse word *klubba*. English contains many words of
Norse origin, dating from the ninth century A.D., when Norwe-
gian and Danish Vikings raided England at will and even set up
kingdoms there. *Sky, egg,* and *window* are a few of the words we
got from the Danes and Norsemen. *Club* is another.

Of course, the club is far older than the Norsemen. It is probably man's most ancient weapon. Clubs may even have been used
by man's ancestors more than a million years ago, before they
were fully human.

In medieval Europe, the club was the main weapon of the
peasants. Strict laws forbade them to carry swords or spears,
which they might use against their cruel rulers. In time of war,
peasants who were forced to serve in their lords' armies often
carried clubs with long nails driven through their heads so that
the points stuck out on the other side. From the peasant's spiked
club developed the spike-headed iron mace, a weapon much
used by knights.

A very popular weapon of medieval England was the *quarter-staff*, a stout pole of oak or other wood from 6 to 9 feet long and a little less than 2 inches thick. Its ends were often bound with iron bands. The quarterstaff was held with your hands near the middle, about shoulder width apart. One theory claims that the user's left hand was one-quarter of the way up from the end; hence the name *quarterstaff*. There is no proof of this, however, and the theory seems to be a fancy of Samuel Johnson, a bril-

liant but crotchety English philosopher and lexicographer of the 1700's. The quarterstaff went out of use in the late 1600's.

A *cudgel* was a short, thick club. Cudgels must have been used in many taproom brawls, for "to take up the cudgels" for someone meant to take his side. In country districts of England, cudgel matches were held until the early 1800's. *Cudgel* comes from an Anglo-Saxon word, *cycgel*, which doesn't seem to be related to anything else.

In Ireland the traditional club was the *shillelagh*, a cudgel of oak or blackthorn which could also be used as a walking stick. The shillelagh (pronounced *shillailey*) is named for a village in the southeast of Ireland, where presumably the best trees for making cudgels grew.

Clubs are used for special purposes today. In many countries the policemen carry short clubs called nightsticks or billies. In India, policemen are armed with long bamboo poles called *lathis*, which resemble the old English quarterstaff.

Club comes from the same root as *clump*, and thus it took on the meaning of gathering together into a mass. As early as 1632 an English writer mentioned people "clubbing" together, that is, combining to achieve a purpose. By 1670, *club* had acquired its modern meaning of a group of people who meet or combine for pleasure or any other purpose.

The clubs you see on playing cards are actually not clubs but clover leaves. In the 1500's, Italian playing cards used a club as the symbol of one of the four suits, while French cards used a trefoil, or clover leaf, for the corresponding suit. English card-players combined the Italian name with the French symbol. As the peasant's weapon, clubs are the lowest-ranking of the four suits. Highest-ranking are spades, whose name comes from *spada*, the Italian word for "sword." As the aristocratic weapon of the knights, spades naturally outranked the plebeian clubs.

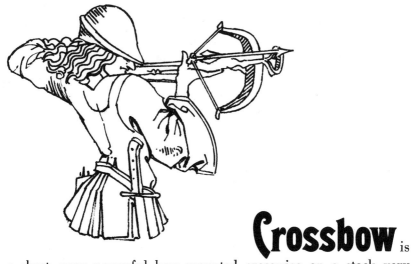

Crossbow is

a short, very powerful bow mounted crosswise on a stock very like the stock of a gun; hence its name. An older name for the crossbow is *arbalest,* which comes from the Latin word *arcuballista* (from *arcus,* "bow," plus *ballista,* "a kind of catapult").

The crossbow fired a heavy, metal-headed arrow called a *bolt* or a *quarrel.* The term *quarrel* comes ultimately from the medieval Latin word *quarrellus,* "a little square" (quarrels were made with chunky, four-sided heads). Power to send the quarrel crashing through a suit of armor at a range of a couple of hundred feet was provided by the bow, which was built up of several layers of tough, springy wood, usually backed with horn or sinew or, later, by spring steel.

Originally, crossbows were spanned (that is, the string was drawn back to shooting position) by the bowman's putting his foot in a stirrup at the end of the stock and yanking the bowstring up with both his hands. Later the string was slipped over a hook on a belt around the bowman's waist, and he forced the bow down with his foot. But by the 1300's crossbows had become so powerful that no normal man had the strength to span one. Instead, mechanical aids were used. Small crossbows had a lever that pulled back the string, while the larger ones had a windlass or a geared device called a *cranequin.* Once pulled back, the string was held in place by a trigger that the bowman pulled to release the arrow.

The crossbow was held and aimed much like a gun. In the hands of a skilled bowman, it was an accurate weapon. However, it was also a very slow weapon because it took a long time to crank it into readiness for each shot. This limited its usefulness in battle. You needed a whole company of crossbowmen, so that while some were reloading, their comrades could protect them. Eventually the crossbow was largely replaced by the much faster-shooting, cheaper, and equally powerful longbow, a British invention, and by the gun, which was inaccurate but required little skill to use.

The crossbow was invented in the fourth century B.C., but it did not become popular until the tenth century A.D., although it was far superior in strength and accuracy to the old-fashioned short bow.

Despite opposition by knights, who disliked its armor-piercing potential, and the Catholic Church, which ineffectually banned it in 1139 (except against infidels), its use spread. Since it was expensive to make, the crossbow was a "gentleman's weapon." In Spain an elite corps of crossbowmen was formed from young men of socially prominent families.

Mercenary soldiers also fancied the crossbow—it enabled them to do most of their fighting at a distance. The northern Italians, particularly the men of Genoa, became specialists in crossbow warfare, and most respectable armies of the thirteenth and fourteenth centuries included a well-paid corps of Genoese crossbowmen.

The downfall of the crossbow began with the famous Battle of Crécy, in 1346. As the battle began, Genoese bowmen hired by the French army faced English archers armed with longbows, while the heavily armored knights of both sides waited behind the lines for their turn at slaughter. The English longbowmen were able to send off five or six arrows for every one the Genoese could launch. Hopelessly outclassed, the crossbowmen broke ranks and fled, to be slaughtered by the infuriated knights of their own side. While this diversion was going on, the English archers were able to pick off several hundred French knights. Although the English were vastly outnumbered, they won a smashing victory. After Crécy, military leaders gradually began switching from the crossbow to more effective types of projectile launchers.

Nevertheless, the crossbow continued to be used on a limited scale in some rural districts of Europe until the mid-seventeenth century and in parts of China until 1860. It is used for hunting by a few enthusiasts today.

Cutlass _{was}

a short, broad sword with a slightly curved blade, used as a side-arm by sailors. The cutlass is basically a small saber. Like other curve-bladed swords, it is designed for slashing rather than for thrusting.

The name *cutlass* is an English version of the French *coutelas*, from *coutel*, or "knife." The ending *-as* carried the idea of large size, so *coutelas* meant "big knife." *Coutel* (*couteau* in modern French) is derived from the Latin *cultellus*, or "little knife," which comes from *culter*, meaning "knife," "razor," or "plow-share."

Cutlass first appeared in English at the end of the 1500's, but the weapon itself must have been around for some time before then. For a while there were two alternate forms of the name, *curtelace* and *curtal-axe*. Some scholars think that these names were attempts by ignorant men to imitate the old Latin word *cultellus*. At any rate, they have not been used for many years.

In the days of sailing ships, the final stage of a battle at sea often involved sailors from one ship leaping onto the deck of another ship and capturing it in fierce hand-to-hand fighting. In this sort of combat, with crowds of men surging back and forth on the cramped deck of a ship, heaving and pitching on the waves, the short, compact cutlass was very handy, whereas a long sword would have got in the way. For nearly 300 years the cutlass, or a weapon much like it, was used by seamen.

But naval tactics changed along with ship design, and by the time of the American Civil War it was no longer practical to send a boarding party leaping onto the deck of an enemy ship. They would have been cut down by a hail of rifle bullets before they got very far. And so the cutlass, like the boarding party, passed into history.

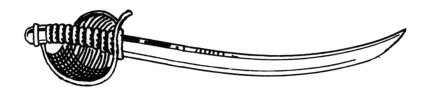

NAVAL CUTLASS

Dagger is

a short knife used for thrusting and stabbing. The name *dagger* goes back to the Middle English period (1150–1450). One medieval Englishman, writing in 1348, noted that some of the noble ladies attending a tournament wore little knives that they called *daggerios* dangling from their girdles, so we know the word is at least that old. Daggers themselves, of course, date back to prehistoric times.

The origin of the name *dagger* is a mystery. The *Oxford English Dictionary* suggests that it comes from an old word, *dag*, meaning "to stab or pierce with a pointed instrument." But the origin of *dag* is not known, either, so that is not much help for the word detective. Language scholars believe there is a connection between *dagger* and the French word *dague* ("dagger") and the German word *Degen* ("a kind of sword"), but it is hard to tell which of these words is the oldest.

In the Middle Ages, a dagger called the *miséricorde* (French for "compassion") was used by knights. The favored technique was to slide it through the joints in an opponent's armor and into the opponent himself. The miséricorde supposedly received its name either because the threat of this dreaded weapon caused men to beg their opponents to have compassion on them or (more likely) because it was used to put a badly wounded opponent out of his misery.

Another dagger that was popular during the Middle Ages was the Italian *cinquedea* (from *cinque diti*, meaning "five fingers"). The cinquedea had a broad, V-shaped blade that was approximately five fingers wide at the hilt; hence the name.

Around the middle of the 1500's dueling with swords became highly fashionable. The dagger took on an additional job, as a duelist's defensive weapon. The duelist held his sword in his right hand and his dagger in his left, using it to parry the thrusts and slashes of his opponent's sword. Special dueling daggers were invented. These had deep notches in the blade, in which you could catch your opponent's sword and break it off with a clever twist of the wrist. Another dueling dagger had a blade that sprang open into a three-pronged fork when a button was pressed. It, too, was a good sword catcher.

There were many types of dagger, each with its own name. The *dirk*, the *poniard*, and the *stiletto* were three well-known ones. They are discussed in separate entries.

"To look daggers" at someone is to express anger and hatred with your look. This pointed expression goes back to the late 1500's and was used by Shakespeare.

THIS SCOTTISH CLANSMAN
WEARS A DIRK ON HIS BELT.

Dirk was

a type of dagger worn by Scottish Highlanders. The name first appeared in print shortly after 1600. It was then spelled *dork*. Later the spelling *durk* was common. The present spelling was the creation of Samuel Johnson, the noted English scholar, who used it in his great dictionary published in 1755. Johnson, a brilliant but eccentric man, had a strong prejudice against the Scots, and he may have altered the spelling of this word to make it seem less Scottish and more English.

The origin of the name *dirk* is not known. Some scholars believe it is a corruption of *Dolch*, the German word for "dagger," but this has never been proved. The Scottish name for "dirk" was *biodag*; it is hard to see how this could have been turned into *dirk*.

In Scotland the dirk became part of the national costume, and it is still worn for ceremonial occasions. The handle of the dirk is traditionally decorated with cairngorms (a yellow or smoky-brown semiprecious stone), and the sheath is bound with silver. Two small knives are often carried in the sheath; presumably they once served as eating implements, while the dirk itself was reserved for the serious business of fighting.

SPANISH HALBERDIER

Halberd was

a foot soldier's weapon during the late Middle Ages. A halberd was basically a battle-ax on the end of a 6-foot pole, but it had extra features that made it more effective against a man in armor. The heavy blade was shaped like a butcher's cleaver, and a powerful man could cut right through a helmet with it, stunning the wearer, if not killing him outright. In addition, the back of the head bore a vicious spike or hook, which could be used to punch into a mounted man's armor and drag him off his horse. The top edge of the halberd was forged into a long, tapering point like a spearhead, enabling the weapon to be used like a spear also. To top it off, halberds were often made with a second spearpoint at the butt end of the shaft.

The halberd, which was used as early as the 1200's, was probably a Swiss invention—at least, it was a Swiss specialty for a couple of hundred years. Today the Swiss are known as a peace-loving, neutral nation, but in the Middle Ages they were feared all over Europe as fierce, brutal warriors. The halberd was one of the weapons that helped them gain that reputation.

By the 1400's the halberd was one of the most common infantry weapons in Europe, and it remained in use until soldiers stopped wearing body armor, in the late 1500's.

The halberd belonged to a family of weapons known as *pole* or *staff arms* because of their long shafts. Other well-known pole arms were the BILL (a kind of glorified brush hook) and the PIKE (a very long spear). Both of these are described separately.

The name *halberd* is an English version of the French *hallebarde*, which in turn comes from a medieval German word, *Helmbarde*. The *Helm* part of this word is simply the German for "helmet." *Barde* was a German name for a "broad ax," and it was derived from an old Germanic word that meant "beard." Presumably the ax was nicknamed "beard" because of its shape, and the name stuck. So a *Helm-barde* was a "helmet-ax"—that is, an ax for smashing helmets, a name that described its function perfectly. In English, *halberd* dates from just before 1500, so it is safe to guess that the English added the halberd to their stock of weapons rather late in the game.

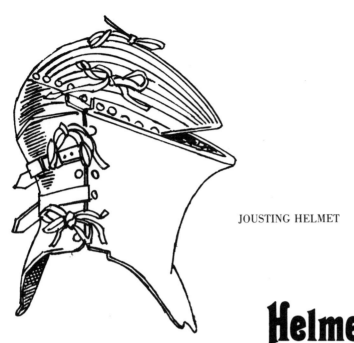

JOUSTING HELMET

Helmet comes

from an ancient Indo-European root, *kel,* meaning "to cover" or "to hide." In Old Germanic, one of the ancestors of English, this became *helmoz,* and in Anglo-Saxon it was *helm,* a word which is still used by poets and writers striving for an archaic effect. (A ship's helm, or steering mechanism, comes from a different origin, an Old Norse word meaning "handle.")

In the late 400's a German-speaking people called the Franks overran much of France and established themselves as rulers. In addition to naming the country after themselves, they gave many Germanic words to the French language. One of these was *helm* (in modern French, *heaume*).

Both the French and the Germans like to call things "little," and the Old French for "little helm" was *helmet.* Since the ruling class of England followed the lead of France in language and fashions for several hundred years, they picked up the word and made it a permanent part of the language.

51

Primitive peoples often wore helmets decorated with animals' horns or teeth. They may have done this partly to look fierce and terrify their enemies, and partly to obtain magically some of the fighting qualities of the animals whose horns and teeth they used. The ancient Celtic and German warriors of Europe used the horns of wild bulls and the tusks of wild boars to decorate their helmets, as did the Vikings later on. Early Japanese samurai (knights) wore stags' antlers on their helmets.

It was in medieval Europe that helmets reached the height of their development. At first, they were simple, conical or kettle-shaped metal head covers, sometimes with a flap sticking down to protect the wearer's nose. But as knighthood and chivalry developed, helmets became more elaborate.

First the helmet was given flaps to cover the back of the wearer's neck—a vulnerable spot—and his cheeks. Then the cheek flaps were extended until they covered the wearer's whole face, with just a couple of narrow slits left open to see out of and to let in air. But even the knights, who were mostly tough, brutish fighters who prided themselves on the amount of discomfort they could endure, realized that this was impractical. They could not get enough air to breathe. And so the visored helmet was invented. This had a movable visor that covered the knight's face and could be swung up out of the way whenever the knight was not actually fighting. In this way, the knight could see and breathe normally.

One of the most bizarre helmets was the great tilting helm, worn only for tournaments. It was made of extra-thick metal and was far too heavy to wear in battle. In addition, the wearer could see out only through a narrow slit at the top of the helmet, which looked rather like a frog's mouth. It is believed that the viewing slit was placed in this awkward position to help the knight aim his lance. Only when the lance tip was held at the

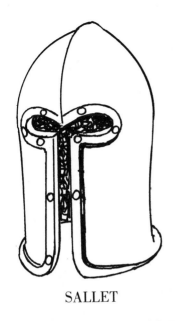

SALLET

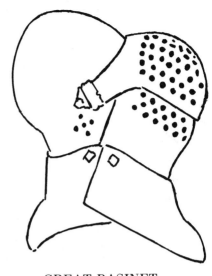

GREAT BASINET

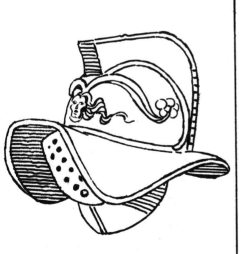

GLADIATOR

ORNAMENTAL, RENAISSANCE

correct height, not too high and not too low, could he see it. In a tilting contest, when both knights rode down a fixed path on either side of a barrier, this limited vision did not matter. In a battle, it would have been fatal.

Tilting helms weighed from 12 pounds up to almost 20 pounds—more than an average-sized Christmas turkey weighs. Imagine carrying that on your head! Helmets used in real fighting weighed from $4\frac{1}{2}$ to 8 or 9 pounds. Of course, only the wealthier knights could afford elaborate helmets. Poor knights had to be content with simpler, cheaper models. Foot soldiers wore leather helmets until they could get a metal one off the corpse of an enemy.

As firearms came into general use, the helmet was gradually given up, except for special troops such as cavalry regiments of some countries. But in World War I trench warfare made it necessary to bring the helmet back again, and combat soldiers have worn it ever since.

In World War I, German soldiers wore helmets with a spike on top. Allied propagandists said that this was so that they could charge with heads lowered and gore anyone in their path. This was not true, but it made wonderful propaganda. The Kaiser (emperor) of Germany did nothing to discourage the rumors, for he felt that they filled his enemies with terror and weakened their will to resist the fierce German warriors.

Javelin was

a short, lightweight spear for throwing at an opponent. The most famous javelin users of the ancient world were the Romans, whose soldiers carried javelins as part of their standard equipment.

The *pilum*, as the Roman javelin was called, had a 7-inch iron head on a 20-inch iron stem, fastened to a wooden shaft. The whole weapon was a bit under 7 feet long. In battle, the Roman soldier would hurl his javelin at his opponent's shield. The weight of the javelin would drag the shield down, and its dangling shaft would make it impossible to maneuver the shield. With his enemy left open, the Roman would then close in with his sword, with which he was an expert. The javelin could also be used at close quarters for thrusting and stabbing, as a bayonet is used today.

The Roman pilum was copied by some of the barbarian peoples who dwelled along the Roman frontier, and these groups continued to use it as they took over the crumbling Roman Empire.

The name *javelin* does not come from the Romans, however. It is a French word dating from the early 1500's, and it is believed to come from a Celtic word, *gavel* or *javel*, meaning a kind of hook. How *hook* became *spear* no one has yet figured out.

In the Middle Ages, the javelin went out of use in warfare. A throwing spear could not possibly match the range of a bow and arrow, and it was not effective against the body armor in use by then. However, in England the javelin lingered on in a limited type of civilian use. The county and borough sheriffs had troops of official guards armed with javelins to accompany them on their rounds and also to act as bodyguards for the judges when court was in session.

The javelin had a revival when the Olympic Games were instituted. Javelin throwing had been a feature of the ancient Greek athletic contests on which the modern Olympics were patterned, and it was included in the pentathlon, the five all-around feats that each contestant must perform in one day. As a major Olympic event, javelin throwing became one of the internationally recognized track sports. The world's record as of this writing is 304 feet 1½ inches, set by Jorma Kinnunen in 1969.

Knife is

one of man's earliest weapons. Uncounted thousands of years
ago, men learned how to chip little flakes off the edge of a sliver
of flint to produce a sharp edge. This was the beginning of the
knife. The knife has been as much a tool as a weapon, but it is
as a weapon that we will consider it here.

Flint knives were not much use in hunting, except for skinning animals and cutting up the meat. But they were good weapons for hand-to-hand fighting. When man learned how to work
metals, knives were among the first things to be made of metal. A
stone knife will take a sharp edge, but it is brittle. A metal knife
lasts much longer.

In fighting, men learned that a long knife might give a man the advantage over his opponent, and blades grew longer until the knife turned into the sword. As a matter of fact, the oldest swords look just like the knives of their time, except that they are bigger.

There is no really satisfactory way of deciding whether a weapon is a large knife or a small sword. The experts disagree in many cases. It is really a matter of opinion.

Many specialized forms of the knife were developed, in addition to the sword. Daggers, cutlasses, machetes, and bayonets are just a few. Some knives took very odd shapes. The Malay *kris*, for example, has a zigzag blade that looks like a writhing snake.

Knife comes from the Anglo-Saxon word *cnif* and can be traced back to an old Germanic root, *knibaz*. *Knife* was once pronounced "kuh-NEEF," but its pronunciation changed by 1500.

A knife familiar to any reader of tales about the Old West is the *Bowie knife*, used by frontiersmen, trappers, and hunters. A long hunting knife, it had a 15-inch blade with a curved tip, and it was as handy for skinning animals as it was for attack or defense in a sudden brawl. It was named for Colonel James Bowie, a hero of the Texan war of independence, who died at the Alamo in 1836. It is not known whether Bowie actually invented the knife that bears his name, but he certainly used it enthusiastically and made it popular.

The hot-tempered settlers of Arkansas used the Bowie knife so much that it was nicknamed the "Arkansas toothpick," and an old nickname for Arkansas was "the Bowie state."

Knife appears in a number of popular and once-popular expressions. For example, "to knife" someone means to harm that person by means of an underhanded trick. This is probably derived from the expression "to knife in the back," which symbolizes a treacherous attack. To English criminals of the early 1800's, "Knife it!" meant "Get out of here as fast as you can!"

Lance is

a type of spear formerly used by cavalry. The name comes from the Old French *lance*, which was derived from the Latin *lancea*, "a light spear."

The lance was not much used in antiquity. The great cavalry fighters of the ancient world, the Persians, relied mainly on massive volleys of arrows from their short, powerful bows, although they sometimes used short lances in a charge. The lance really came into its own with the rise of knighthood in medieval Europe. For several centuries armor-clad knights on horseback, armed with lances, dominated Europe's battlefields, much as tanks do today.

The lance was the chief weapon used in the famous tournaments of the Middle Ages. Tournaments began in the eleventh century as unregulated free-for-all brawls between any number of knights, and contestants were often killed or injured. But later the tournament was refined and standardized and conducted according to strict rules, so that the risk of death or serious injury was almost eliminated. Tournaments could include fights between knights on foot armed with swords or maces, but the main feature was always the joust, an encounter between one or more pairs of knights on horseback with lances.

Joust comes from an Old French word, *juster* or *jouster*, which is derived from a Latin word, *juxtare*, meaning "to approach" or "to meet." When the knights met, the objective of each was to knock the other fellow off his horse or at least to hit him hard enough to break his lance. In keeping score, points were awarded according to where the opponent was struck, and a jouster could lose points for hitting his opponent's saddle. To make it a little easier to score points, special hollow lances made of soft wood were used. These broke easily, unlike the sturdy battle lance, and gave the aristocratic spectators a better show.

For safety's sake, blunt-tipped lances were used in most jousts by the thirteenth century, although jousts might be fought with sharp lances on request. By the fourteenth century jousting lances usually were tipped with three or four blunt prongs to spread out the impact, so that the risk of their going through a contestant's armor was almost zero.

Jousting was done in a large, enclosed area called the *lists* (from *liste*, a word used in both Anglo-Saxon and Old French to mean "boundary"). In the fifteenth century a safety device called the *tilt* was added. This was a barrier 5 or 6 feet high, which ran from one end of the lists to the other to keep the knights and their horses from colliding. Originally the tilt was a heavy cloth hung from a rope; in fact, its name comes from the French word for "cloth," *toile*. But the cloth was soon replaced by a stout barricade of wood, which the knights could not push aside or run their spears through. In time, *tilting* came to be a synonym for *jousting*. "Running at full tilt" meant rushing ahead as fast as you could go, like a knight trying to get up enough momentum to knock his opponent off his horse.

Despite the popularity of tournaments and jousting, the lance disappeared from warfare around 1600. The reason was that firearms had become so powerful that bulletproof armor was too

POLISH LANCER
OF THE GUARD

heavy to wear. And without armor a lancer was too vulnerable. But it was revived by Polish and Cossack cavalrymen in the late eighteenth century, and Napoleon used lancers very effectively in the early nineteenth century. During the nineteenth century, most European countries equipped their cavalry with lances again, and some maintained special lancer regiments. Dressed in elegant uniforms and bearing distinctive names such as Hussars and Uhlans, the lancers were the cream of the elite troops.

Although mechanized warfare made the lance obsolete, Poland's cavalry was still using the lance at the outbreak of World War II. As might be expected, the gallant Polish lancers were no match for German tanks and machine guns.

A "free-lancer" is anyone who sells his services to all bidders. Today this term refers especially to artists and writers. It was created around 1820 by the British novelist Sir Walter Scott. Scott was referring to a class of professional soldiers that flourished during the Middle Ages. These men were poor knights— younger sons of aristocratic families who could not hope to inherit their families' wealth. These men hired themselves, and their lances, out to the highest bidder, for they owed allegiance to no master.

Mace was

the knight's version of the crude club of the peasant. The mace, $2\frac{1}{2}$ to 3 feet long, originally had a metal head and a wooden handle; later it was made entirely of metal. The head of the mace was studded with projections of various shapes.

The mace was used mostly for fighting on horseback. It could shock or stun even a man protected by plate armor, and a few unusually powerful knights could actually smash armor plate with a blow of the mace. A man clad in flexible chain mail could have his bones broken by the mace, and an unarmored man must have suffered frightful wounds.

Mace comes from *masse* or *mace*, an Old French word for a "sledgehammer," derived from *mattea*, a Latin word for "club." In modern French it is called *masse d'armes*, or "weapon sledgehammer." Maces were used by the Normans when they invaded England in 1066. A famous tapestry shows Bishop Odo, a warlike Norman churchman, fighting with a mace so that he would not break the rule that forbade churchmen to shed blood. Apparently it was all right for the bellicose bishop to crush a Saxon's skull if it could be managed bloodlessly.

During the era of chivalry, maces developed a fantastic variety of designs, but they went out of use in the sixteenth century. The mace did survive on a very limited scale, however, as a ceremonial object. A number of English cities owned beautifully decorated silver maces which were displayed at meetings of the city councils. As symbols of power, these maces were also carried before the city fathers in civic processions. One of the most famous maces is the one that belongs to the British House of Commons. This mace, which rests upon a table in front of the Speaker of the House, has been used since 1660. By tradition, Parliament can do no business unless the mace is in its proper place.

Pike was

a very long spear used by foot soldiers in the fifteenth, sixteenth, and seventeenth centuries. A pike had a heavy steel point mounted on a shaft 16 to 20 feet long. In battle formation, pikemen stood in a compact mass facing the enemy, three or more ranks deep. The front rank was armed with 16-foot pikes, the second rank with 18-footers, and the third rank with 20-footers, so that they presented an even front to the oncoming enemy. It must have taken an exceptionally strong man to handle a 20-foot pike, especially with the weight of another man, or a horse and rider, rushing against it.

The pike may have been invented by the Swiss; at any rate, they were the first to use it on a large scale. Swiss foot soldiers armed with pikes won some notable battles against the heavily armored cavalry of Austria. The great advantage of the pike was that it kept your enemy at a safe distance from you while you skewered him. It was especially good against cavalry, since you could disable a mounted knight's horse with it, and your comrades could take care of the knight himself when he regained his feet—which he might not if the horse fell on him. The pike could also slide between the joints of armor and damage the person inside the steel shell.

After some costly defeats, the Austrians adopted the pike, and soon it was used throughout Europe. Firearms did not entirely replace the pike until the late seventeenth century—in fact, up to then arquebusiers and musketeers needed pikemen to guard them while they were reloading their guns.

PIKEMAN, 1587

Pike comes from the French word *piquer*, "to prick or pierce." It goes back to an old Germanic root carrying the idea of something sharp or pointed. To an Englishman, *pike* could mean a haystack with a pointed top (for shedding rain), a pickax, a spike, a thorn, a point, or a hill with a pointed top. The word *peak* may also come from the same root. The fish we call *pike* probably received its name because of the pointy shape of its jaws.

A *turnpike* was originally a spiked barricade placed across a road or path to bar attackers. Later it came to mean any barrier across a road. About 1750 some enterprising people in England got the idea of building private roads and charging travelers a fee to use them. The entrances to these roads were barred by gates or turnpikes. Thus they received the name of *turnpike roads*, or *turnpikes*, for short. Since turnpike roads were kept in much better shape than the public roads, they always had plenty of business, in spite of their fees.

Poniard was

not a cavalryman mounted on a pony, but a kind of dagger much used in swift and stealthy murders in sixteenth- and seventeenth-century Europe. The poniard was short and sharp-pointed, easily concealed beneath the flowing cloak of a courtier, and always ready for a sudden stab at an opportune moment.

Writers and dramatists, Shakespeare among them, were fascinated by the poniard's sinister reputation. It became a convention to equip villains of stories and plays with poniards. Authors of historical novels still follow this tradition.

Poniard comes from the Old French name for this weapon, *poignard* or *poignal*, derived from *poing*, the French word for "fist." (To deliver a stroke with this wicked little dagger, you clenched your fist around the handle and used an overhand motion.)

Poing comes from the Latin word for "fist," *pugnus*, which is also related to the modern word *pugilist*, a refined synonym for a professional boxer. Fortunately, boxers are armed with padded gloves, not with poniards, or their careers would be short.

Saber <small>is</small>

a type of sword with a long, gently curved blade with one sharp edge. Designed for cutting and thrusting, the saber was used almost entirely by cavalrymen.

The word *saber* came into English about 1680 from the French *sabre*, and the English still use the French spelling. The weapon itself had been introduced to France by German mercenaries, who called it a *Sabel* or *Säbel*. The name may be derived from a Polish name for a sword of that type, *szabla*, or the Hungarian name, *szablya*.

The saber may have been developed from the sweeping, curve-bladed swords used by Turkish cavalrymen in the late Middle Ages. By 1500 the Turks had overrun a good part of southeastern and central Europe, and Hungarians and Poles battled them for another century and a half. Europeans may have attributed the success of the Turks to the design of their swords, rather than to their skill and ferocity. But, whatever its origin, the saber became a major cavalry weapon, and it was used down to the American Civil War and even later.

In the early 1800's, a lightweight version of the saber became popular for fencing. Students at German universities developed a very unpleasant version of dueling with sabers, which they called *Mensur*. In this sport, the two contenders stood at a measured distance from each other—the word *Mensur* itself comes from the Latin word for "measurement"—and were not allowed to move their feet. In fact, they were not supposed to move any part of their bodies except their sword arms. When the referee shouted *"Los!"* they started slashing away at each other's heads, the object being to see who could score the most wounds on the other person's face. The blood flowed freely, but the duelers were protected by heavy padding almost everywhere but on their faces, so serious injuries were not common. After the fight, everyone would go off and get drunk together at the German equivalent of the fraternity house.

Saber scars on a German student's face were supposed to be a proof of manhood and bravery. They were also a proof of social status, since university students then were almost all sons of the nobility or of rich middle-class families. It is rumored that some students who didn't want to go through the painful ritual of the *Mensur* bribed doctors to make false dueling scars on their faces by plastic surgery.

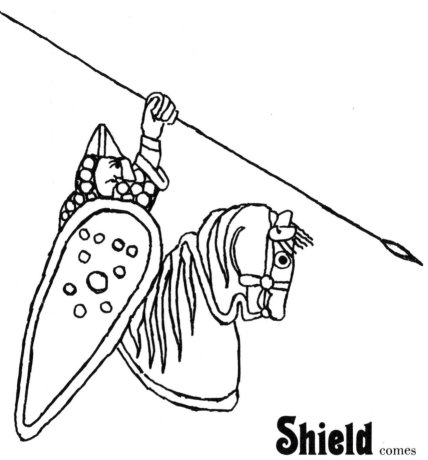

Shield comes

from the Anglo-Saxon *sceld*, which may come from a Germanic root, *skelduz*, that scholars think meant "board." The shield is a very ancient protective device, even older than armor.

The first shields were probably made of rawhide (untreated animal skin) stretched over a framework of sticks. Rawhide dries almost as hard as wood, and a thick layer of rawhide must have given good protection against spears, stones, and arrows. Later in man's history, shields were made of wood, often covered with leather, or of metal. But the rawhide shield was still being used by the armies of the Zulu and other warlike African tribes in the late 1800's.

Shields were made in almost every imaginable shape and size. The ancient Greeks described in Homer's poems, for example, carried shields shaped like a figure eight and long enough to cover them from neck to feet. Many ancient peoples used long, straight-sided shields. When soldiers armed with such shields lined up side by side, with the edges of their shields over-lapping, the effect was like a wall. Such big shields were proba-bly meant for protection against showers of darts, arrows, and spears. They would not have been much use in hand-to-hand fighting, as they were hard to maneuver with.

For hand-to-hand combat, smaller shields were used, covering approximately the area from shoulder to knee. The Roman legionaries used leather shields of about this size, strengthened with a heavy metal plate in the center. The metal plate, decorated with the symbol of the legionary's unit, was also good for bash-ing an enemy.

When the Normans conquered England, in 1066, the defend-ing Saxon army had round shields, while the Norman invaders had narrow shields shaped something like a round-topped kite, tapering down to a point at the bottom. During the Middle Ages, a small, round shield called a *buckler* was popular. The buckler measured perhaps a foot across. You held it at arm's length and used it to block or deflect your opponent's blows.

In the mid-1500's, about the time Queen Elizabeth came to the throne of England, the term *swashbuckler* was coined to describe the kind of person who banged his sword on his shield to make a big noise and intimidate people. A swashbuckler was thus a swaggering bully, a type of which there was no scarcity in Elizabethan times.

In ancient times, successful warriors often decorated their shields lavishly, to show off their power and the wealth they had taken from conquered enemies. A famous leader's shield seemed to fascinate people, just as a famous football player's custom-made car does today. In the *Iliad*, the ancient Greek poet Homer described in the most minute detail the decorations of the hero Achilles' shield, and for hundreds of lines he discussed how the shield had been made. Up in Viking country, Scandinavian bards chanted similar admiring descriptions of the fabulous shields of Norse heroes. This was perhaps natural in societies where war was the chief escape from boredom and poets earned their keep by singing the praises of fighting men.

A knight of the Middle Ages had his coat of arms painted on his shield to announce his identity to all comers. This was necessary because in a battle the knights' faces were concealed by their helmets, and it was impossible to tell friend from foe. By glancing at the insignia on the shield, you could tell whether the knight galloping toward you was going to help you or attack you.

The Latin word for "shield" was *scutum*. In Norman French this became *escuchon*, and in English it became *escutcheon*. A knight who had disgraced himself was said to have a "blot on his escutcheon."

Another old word for "shield" was *target*, derived from the Old Norse word *targa*. The target was a small, lightweight shield like the buckler, and it was used especially by infantrymen and archers. In archery practice, a dummy target made of cloth stuffed with straw was set up for the bowmen to shoot at, and in time *target* came to mean something to aim at. Its original meaning of "shield" was entirely forgotten except by writers of historical novels.

GRECIAN WARRIOR

Spear hardly
needs a definition. Next to the club and the knife, the spear is
probably man's oldest weapon. From the spear came a whole
family of weapons, such as the javelin, the pike, and the lance.
The arrow, too, is derived from the spear. It is a little spear
launched from a bow.

The earliest spears were probably no more than long, more-or-less straight sticks with one end sharpened and hardened in a fire. Later, man learned how to make points of bone, horn, and stone, which improved the spear's penetrating power. Sometimes other materials were used, depending on what people had on hand. On some islands of the Pacific Ocean, the native peoples tipped their spears with razor-sharp sharks' teeth. When man learned how to work with metals, spearheads were made of copper, then bronze, and then iron.

Ancient peoples had many types of spears, but they fell into three main classes. There were short spears for throwing and long spears for close-in fighting. There was also a medium-length spear, 6 or 7 feet long, that was used for both purposes.

The Greeks armed most of their soldiers with spears, and the Romans also used spears as a main weapon. The Romans at first used a long spear called a *hasta*, but later they changed over to the deadly *pilum*, a javelin.

Spears were used all through the Middle Ages. The PIKE, a very long spear, was an infantry weapon until the late 1600's. The LANCE, a long spear used by mounted men, was used as late as 1939 by the Polish cavalry in their gallant but futile resistance to the German armored divisions that roared across the border and started World War II.

Spear comes from the Anglo-Saxon *spere*. This may have been derived from an ancient root that carried the idea of a wooden beam. In Europe, ash was the wood preferred for making spears because it is strong and springy and does not break easily.

To a German, a spear is a *Speer*; to a Frenchman it is a *lance* or *javelot*. A Spanish speaker would call it a *lanza* or *venablo*. In the Scandinavian languages, the names for a spear are related to the English word *spit* (in the sense of a pointed rod for roasting meat on).

Stiletto was

a short, slender Italian dagger much favored by assassins. The name is a diminutive form of *stilo*, one of the many Italian terms for a "dagger." It is derived from *stilus*, the Latin name for a pointed sliver of bone, wood, or metal used for writing on wax tablets. It is probable that the shape of the stiletto blade reminded people of the Roman *stilus*. *Stiletto* came into use in English not long after 1600, a time at which Englishmen were enchanted by all things Italian.

Like the PONIARD, the stiletto was easily concealed beneath one's clothes and was well suited for a treacherous attack. It was used by courtiers, shady characters, and robbers for many years. In the late nineteenth and early twentieth centuries, the stiletto was popular among Italian-American gangsters. Its needle-sharp, three- or four-sided blade slid easily into a victim and left only the slightest of marks when it was pulled out. Furthermore, it made no noise. Thus, it could be used in a crowd without attracting attention.

But a stiletto was not just a weapon; in the nineteenth century the name came to be used for a kind of needle used in embroidery work.

Sword comes

from the Anglo-Saxon *sweord*, which goes back to an old Germanic root, *swerdom*. The words for "sword" in modern Germanic languages still show a close resemblance (close to the language scholar, at any rate). Originally the *w* in *sword* was pronounced, but it became silent long ago.

The ancient Greek word for "sword" was *xiphos*. Forms of this word can be found in the scientific names of many plants and animals, such as *Xiphosura* ("swordtail"), the scientific name of the horseshoe crab.

The Romans had names for at least three kinds of swords. The *ensis* was a primitive type of sword with a blunt tip, good only for chopping away at your opponent. It was replaced by the *gladius*, which became one of the main weapons of the famous Roman legions. It was also the weapon of the gladiators, whose bloody combats were the favorite "sporting" events of the Roman world. The gladius, a short, heavy sword with a sharp point and two cutting edges, originated in Spain, but it was the Romans who made its reputation.

The last of the Roman swords was a long, single-edged weapon called a *spatha*, which came into use rather late in Rome's history. The words for "sword" in several modern languages are descended from the Latin *spatha*: Italian *spada*, Spanish *espada*, French *épée* (worn down from its original form of *espade*).

Italian playing cards of the 1500's used *spade*, or "sword," as the symbol of one of the four suits. English cardplayers took over the name, but in place of the sword design they used a French symbol representing a spearhead. This is the "spade" that cardplayers hold in their hands today.

A sword is basically an outsized knife, and it is really impossible to say at what point a large knife becomes a small sword, or vice versa. The oldest known swords date back to the beginning of the Bronze Age (about 3000 B.C.).

Bronze was the first really satisfactory material man had for making swords. Stone was too difficult to make into a large blade, and besides, a stone sword would snap in two at the first hard blow. It was possible to set small, sharp-edged chips of stone along the edges of a thin wooden blade, as the Aztecs did. This produced a weapon that could deal a wicked slash, but there was always the danger of the stone teeth getting loosened and falling off.

Copper, which man learned to use about 5000 B.C., was all right for knives, but it was too soft and easily bent for swords. But the development of tough, hard bronze (an alloy of copper and tin) made swords practical.

About 1000 B.C. bronze was replaced by iron, which was stronger than bronze and held its edge better. In addition, iron was cheaper to produce and easier to shape. A soldier armed with an iron sword could almost always get the better of one armed with a bronze sword, other things being equal. Eventually steel, which was still harder, tougher, and more resilient, took the place of iron.

Swords have been made in many sizes and shapes, from less than 2 feet to more than 4 feet, not counting the handle. There have been swords for chopping and swords for thrusting and swords that were made to do both. Swords have been straight and curved, single-edged and double-edged.

Some of the better-known swords of history are:

The *broadsword*, a long, heavy chopping sword with a broad blade, usually made for use with two hands. The British used to have a sentimental fondness for the broadsword, which they regarded as a symbol of old-fashioned British pluck and hardihood.

The *claymore* (from the Gaelic *claidheamh mor*, or "great sword"), a double-edged broadsword used by Scottish Highlanders until about 1600. The claymore was one of Scotland's traditional national weapons.

The *falchion*, a single-edged sword with a broad, curved blade. Its name is derived from the Latin *falx*, meaning "sickle," because of its shape. Eventually, *falchion* came to be used carelessly to mean any kind of sword.

The *foil*, a slender, flexible sword with blunt edges and a sharp point which is usually guarded by a blunt button. The foil was invented in France in the late 1600's for use in the extremely popular sport of fencing. With the button removed from its tip, it became a serious dueling weapon. The name probably comes from the Old French *foil*, meaning "leaf," which is derived from the Latin *folium*. It may also come from another Old French word, *foine*, meaning a kind of fishing spear. When the foil was introduced, followers of the old cut-and-slash school of fighting may have compared it derisively to the fish spear.

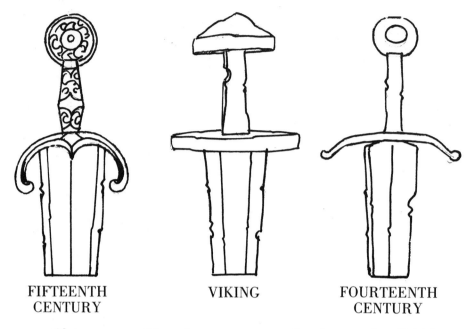

FIFTEENTH
CENTURY

VIKING

FOURTEENTH
CENTURY

Glaive was a fifteenth-century name for the regular British broadsword. In the sixteenth century it was used to mean a lance. In the seventeenth century it changed meanings again, this time to a big knife blade mounted on the end of a long pole. The name comes from an Old French word for "lance."

The *rapier* was a slim, two-edged, pointed sword used mainly for thrusting. An Italian or Spanish invention of the 1500's, it became *the* weapon for dueling. Toward the end of the next century, fashions changed, and the foil became the new favorite for stylish duelists. The name *rapier* comes from the French *rapière*, whose origin is absolutely unknown, although some historians have guessed that it is derived from a word meaning "poker."

The *saber*, a long, single-edged, curved sword, is described in its own entry.

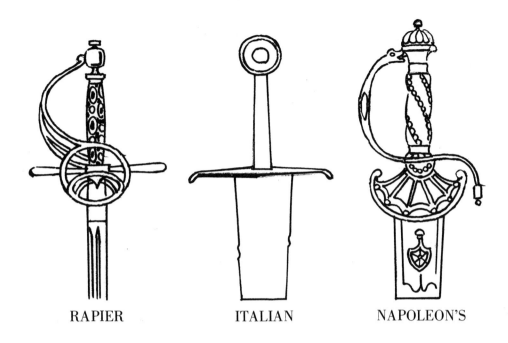

RAPIER   ITALIAN   NAPOLEON'S

The *scimitar* was a short, heavy sword with a blade curved like a crescent moon. An excellent weapon for chopping, it was almost useless for thrusting. The name is probably a European corruption of the Persian name for this sword, *shamshir* or *shimshir*, meaning "lion's claw." The scimitar originated in the Near East and was a traditional weapon in Moslem countries.

In ancient and medieval times, people believed that swords had magical qualities. They could speak, sing, answer questions, and foretell the future. The swords of the great mythical heroes could make their owners invisible, prevent them from being wounded, or unfailingly wound or kill the heroes' antagonists. In some places, the iron or steel blades of swords were considered a charm against witchcraft.

With so many superstitious beliefs about swords, it is no wonder that men considered them almost as living beings and often gave them personal names. Famous swords of legendary heroes are King Arthur's Excalibur and Roland's Durendal.

Swords were treasured and handed down from father to son. This was particularly true in Japan, where the samurai had a semireligious mystique about their swords. Many peoples considered their swords so holy that they would swear oaths on them as we would on the Bible.

The sword appears in so many expressions that it is impossible to list them all. Here are a few.

The "sword of Damocles" is a figure of speech for an extremely perilous situation. It comes from an old Greek legend about a man named Damocles, who was a hanger-on of Dionysius, the dictator of Syracuse (the same ruler mentioned in CATAPULT). Damocles never tired of praising the tyrant and telling him what a wonderful life such a great ruler must have. One day this gushing flattery became too much even for the dictator, so he invited Damocles to share his happiness at dinner. When Damocles sat down, the table was spread with tempting delicacies. Just as he reached for his cup of wine, Dionysius commanded him to look up. Over his head was a sword, suspended by a single hair. "Now," said the tyrant, "you know what it is to be a ruler."

A two-edged sword cuts both ways, and so the expression "a two-edged sword" means any action that can hurt you as much as it can help you.

In the great age of dueling, *blade* was first a synonym for the sword itself and then became a chic, slangy term for a swordsman. A *gay blade* was a carefree, gallant fellow who would never turn down a chance to prove his skill with the sword and was game for any escapade. By and by, however, the gay blade lost his swordsmanship and became simply a playboy.

Part 2

Arquebus was

an early type of firearm. It was one of the first guns designed to be fired with its butt held against the shooter's shoulder. Today we think of this as the normal shooting position, but up to then guns were held with the butt lying on top of the shooter's shoulder, which meant that he had to take the full force of the recoil with his hands, wrists, and arms or else with the butt resting on his chest, which must have knocked the wind out of him.

The arquebus seems to have been a Spanish invention of the late 1400's, but its name comes from a German term, *Hakbühse* or *Hakenbüchse*, meaning "hook gun." It was originally made with a hook on the underside of the barrel which was meant to fit over the top of a wall or other support to take up the recoil of the gun. As the art of gunmaking improved, arquebuses became lighter and easier to handle, and the *Hake*, or hook, disappeared on all but the largest models. Meanwhile, the name had passed into other languages: into French as *harquebuse*; into Italian as *archibugio*; into Spanish as *arcabuzo*. In English it took some strange forms: *hackbush, hagbush, hackbut,* and *hagbutt. Hackbush* dates back at least to 1484. *Arquebus* comes from the French version of the name, and it is sometimes spelled with an *h*, French-style, especially in Britain. It began to be used in English about 1520.

The arquebus was a matchlock gun (see the entry MATCHLOCK for an explanation of how it worked). It was hardly an accurate weapon, but it did not need to be. It was meant to be used by a whole line of soldiers firing together at a line of enemy soldiers. The resulting hail of lead was bound to hit some of the enemy.

The arquebus became so popular with military commanders that at one time *arquebus* was used as the name of any gun light enough to be fired from the shoulder. Toward the end of the 1500's, however, it gave way to the musket, which was a more powerful weapon.

Bayonet is

probably named for the French city of Bayonne, which was, in the Middle Ages, a center for the manufacture of daggers. At first, *bayonet* seems to have been the name of a kind of short dagger made in Bayonne and used by soldiers and civilians alike. But in the early 1600's some inventive soldier devised a dagger whose handle could be stuck into the muzzle of a gun, converting the gun into a spear or pike for hand-to-hand combat. An infantry regiment from Bayonne is believed to have been the first to use the new combination weapon, and *bayonette* (the French spelling) was probably first used as a nickname for the funny-looking daggers that these soldiers stuck in the ends of their guns.

Until the invention of the bayonet, the musketeer was helpless during the time it took to reload his gun after firing it. Each unit of musketeers had to be guarded by a unit of pikemen to keep enemy cavalrymen from galloping down on the musketeers and slashing them to bits with their sabers or skewering them on their lances while they reloaded. The bayonet turned every musketeer into his own pikeman and gave him a better chance of coming through a battle alive. By the late 1600's most European armies had adopted the bayonet.

The original bayonet, or plug bayonet, had a serious fault. As long as is was in place, the muzzle of the gun was plugged up, and the gun could not be fired. A bayonet fitted with loose rings that slipped over the barrel of the gun was tried. This left the muzzle of the gun clear, but it was likely to fall off in combat, just when it was needed. The problem was finally solved by the invention of the socket bayonet around the end of the 1600's. In this type, the blade of the bayonet was attached to a hollow socket, or sleeve, that fitted over the end of the gun barrel. A slot in the side of the sleeve fitted over a stud, or small projection, on the barrel. A half twist of the socket locked the bayonet firmly in place. The socket bayonet, with variations, remained the standard design for nearly 200 years.

Through the 1700's, 1800's, and early 1900's the bayonet charge was looked upon as the climax of battle action. After the enemy had been softened up by musket or rifle fire, the soldiers would fix their bayonets and run toward the enemy lines, trying to drive back the detested foe and take his position. The lines of men in their colorful uniforms, advancing in strict formation with banners flying and bugles blaring, must have been an impressive sight. Meanwhile, the enemy was trying to shoot down as many of the charging soldiers as possible. When armies began using machine guns, a line of advancing soldiers was too easily mowed down, and the battlefield bayonet charge is now a thing of the past.

Blunderbuss was

a type of musket with a short barrel and a very wide bore, and often with a flaring muzzle. The name *blunderbuss* is a corruption of the Dutch word *donderbus*, meaning "thunderbox." It was an apt description of the noise produced when one of these firearms was discharged.

If the name is any indication, the blunderbuss may have been a Dutch invention, but wherever it originated, it became popular all over Europe. The exact date of its invention is not known

—probably sometime between 1620 and 1640. The name first appears in English in the early 1650's.

Although imaginative artists love to portray the Pilgrim colonists of New England armed with blunderbusses, in fact this was just not so. For one thing, the blunderbuss had probably not been invented at the time the *Mayflower* sailed, and it did not come into general use until the late 1600's, half a century after the Pilgrims landed at Plymouth Rock. For another, it would have been of little use under pioneer conditions in the New World, where men needed good hunting weapons. For the blunderbuss was not a hunting weapon or a military weapon. It could not send a ball through a deer—or an Indian raider—at 50 yards. It was strictly a defensive weapon for very close range.

The blunderbuss was designed to hurl a spreading cloud of missiles—usually pistol or musket balls nearly $\frac{3}{4}$ inch in diameter—the idea being that at least one of the balls was almost sure to score a hit if the target was not too far away. Therefore, the blunderbuss was made with a wide bore, which could hold a good-sized load of shot, and a flaring muzzle, which was intended to allow the charge to spread more easily, thus blanketing as large an area as possible with a hail of bone-crushing metal balls. Experience proved that the flare of the muzzle actually had no effect on the spread of the load, and gunmakers gradually reduced the amount of flare until the later models of blunderbuss had an almost straight barrel. Sometimes a slightly flaring muzzle was used, since it made a handy funnel for convenient loading.

In an emergency, a blunderbuss could be loaded with stones, broken glass, or scrap metal. This was not the recommended procedure, however. Such materials could badly scratch the bore of the gun, and if a big chunk of stone or metal got stuck in the bore, the gun could blow up in the shooter's face.

Like its modern descendant the shotgun, the blunderbuss was popular with householders and stagecoach guards. Although inaccurate at any distance, it was lethal in a face-to-face confrontation. Burglars and highway bandits learned a healthy respect for the clumsy-looking weapon.

Blunderbusses were also used on naval ships to repel boarders and to put down mutinies among the crew. No matter how ill treated a seaman might be, he was usually not desperate enough to risk being blown to bits by a blunderbuss. Some naval blunderbusses were made as large as small cannons. Such outsized pieces were far too heavy for a man to hold. They were fitted with swivels and mounted on the gunwale of the ship.

Blunderbusses were manufactured and used up into the early nineteenth century, but their place was soon taken over by the shotgun, an improved form of "scatter-gun" that was good for hunting, as well as for defense.

Bullet comes
from the French word *boulette*, meaning "little ball." For hundreds of years bullets were, in fact, little balls, miniature versions of the ponderous metal balls shot by cannon.

Bullets were not all round at first, however. Men experimented with cone-shaped, egg-shaped, and cylindrical bullets, too, in an effort to find the best shape. Some early guns even shot metal arrows. But around 1550 gun users generally settled on the ball as the most practical shape for a bullet. (Modern bullets are cylindrical, with a round or pointed nose. This shape works best in high-powered rifles.)

Early bullets were made of a variety of materials, including stone, brass, copper, tin, and lead. There were also iron and steel bullets for piercing armor. Eventually lead came to be the standard material. It was easy to melt, so that a shooter could cast his own bullets by his campfire. And it was heavy enough to pack a powerful wallop.

A good deal of picturesque and fanciful folklore grew up around bullets. For example, a silver bullet was thought to have the power to kill vampires, werewolves, and other supernatural, evil creatures that were otherwise invulnerable. Perhaps the white color of silver was associated with purity and was therefore thought to carry God's protection.

Nineteenth-century writers fostered the belief that American Indian warriors, when wounded in battle, would bite on a lead bullet to keep from crying out in pain. In the imaginary world of these talespinners, frontiersmen and soldiers also bit bullets rather than disgrace themselves by a single moan. If anyone tried it in real life, however, he probably added the pain of broken teeth to his suffering.

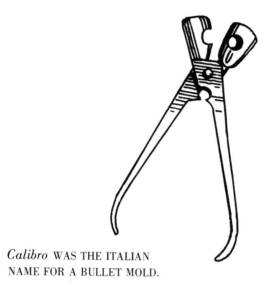

Calibro WAS THE ITALIAN
NAME FOR A BULLET MOLD.

Caliber is

the diameter of a bullet or similar projectile and also the internal
diameter of a gun. Language historians believe that the term
caliber comes ultimately from an Arabic word, *qalib*, meaning
"mold." Italian traders, who did a great deal of business with
the Arabs, may have taken this word back to Italy. At any rate,
Italian gunmakers began to use it, giving it the Italian form of
calibro. They used it to refer to the size of cannonballs and
bullets. From here it was only a step to using *calibro* to denote
the size of the guns that fired these projectiles. The French
adopted this handy technical term, calling it *calibre*. Before the
end of the 1500's it had made its way to England. Incidentally,

the English still prefer the French spelling. The common American spelling, *caliber*, is probably the creation of Noah Webster, the great dictionary maker of the early United States. One of Webster's goals was to make spelling closer to the spoken forms of words. Another was to make American spelling distinct from that of the former enemy, Britain.

Calibers have been measured in a variety of ways. At first they were measured by the weight of the projectile. A cannon, for example, might be classified as a 24-pounder, meaning that it fired a round cast-iron ball of 24 pounds' weight. This system of measurement for artillery pieces lasted well into the 1800's. Musket, rifle, and pistol calibers were also measured by weight. The unit was the "bore"—that is, the number of lead balls the same diameter as the bore of the gun that were needed to make up 1 pound. (*Bore* meant both "the inside of the gun barrel" and "its diameter.") Thus, a 12-bore musket fired a ball weighing 1/12 pound. An 8-bore musket fired a ball weighing $\frac{1}{8}$ pound, or 2 ounces. In modern terms, such a gun would have a caliber of .835 inch. Most muskets did not have such a large caliber— the usual sizes ran from .69 to .80 inch.

Today calibers are measured in fractions of an inch or in millimeters. This system did not come into general use until the mid-1800's. The "bore" system survives in today's shotguns, although nowadays the word *gauge* is used instead of *bore*. In Britain, *bore* is still used for shotguns and large-caliber double-barreled rifles for shooting big game.

Caliber also has a figurative meaning referring to a person's character or the quality of his work. Thus, someone might say, "Desmond is a top-notch lawyer, but he's not of the caliber we need in a Supreme Court judge." A boss might say to an employee, "I'm sorry, Jack, but the caliber of your work does not justify a raise." This use of *caliber* dates back to about 1570.

Cannon is

a word that has changed very little in its travels from one language to another. It began as the Italian *cannone*, meaning "big tube," from *canna*, "a reed or tube." In French it became *canon*. When it reached England from France in the 1520's, it doubled the *n* in the middle of the word. Since that time, cannons have changed almost beyond recognition, but the name has not.

Cannons may be an Italian invention; at least, the earliest written record of their existence is an order from the city of Florence, in northern Italy, for a number of cannons and cannonballs. This document dates from 1326, so we can safely assume that cannons had already been used for some time before then.

The earliest cannons were of two main types. One was shaped like a giant vase or sometimes like a huge soup kettle. The Italians called this type of cannon a *vasa*, or "vase," and the French called it a *pot-de-fer*, or "iron pot." The other type was a long tube, and it was this kind that was named *cannone*.

In the 1400's a number of cannons of mammoth size were built. These giant guns were given names, and they were looked upon almost as if they had living personalities. One of the most renowned of the monster cannons was the Scottish gun Mons Meg, which had a barrel 13 feet 4 inches long and a bore of 20 inches. An even bigger gun was Dulle Griete, or "Crazy Greta," built for the city of Ghent, in what is now Belgium. Dulle Griete's barrel was $16\frac{1}{2}$ feet long and weighed about 13 tons. It measured 33 inches across the mouth and fired a stone cannonball weighing 600 pounds. One of the largest guns ever made was created in 1453 for the Turks to use in besieging Constantinople. This monster, 17 feet long and weighing about 18 tons, was said to be capable of shooting a half-ton stone cannonball for almost a mile.

Such huge guns, of course, could not be used in regular battles. They were much too heavy to be moved about. They were used as siege guns, battering away at the walls of castles and fortified cities from a fixed position. The huge mass of metal was loaded onto a specially built wagon by cranes and dragged to its site by teams of twenty or thirty powerful oxen—more if the gun was especially heavy. At the site, it was hoisted off its wagon and lowered onto a cradle of massive timbers. A heavy timber backstop half-buried in the ground prevented the force of the recoil from pushing the gun off its cradle.

The big siege guns, or *bombards*, as they were called, were set up about 100 yards from the castle they were to knock down. This was well within the range of the defenders' arrows, but the gunners were protected by a heavy, movable wooden shield in front of the gun as they cleaned and loaded their thunderous engine of destruction.

Sometime around the middle 1400's, trunnions were invented. These were metal pivots on either side of the barrel that supported the cannon's weight. With trunnions, the muzzle of the gun could easily be swung up or down to allow for different ranges. Cannons were made lighter and mounted on permanent wheeled carriages for easier transportation.

Guns designed especially for battlefield use, the so-called fieldpieces, came into use. These were of relatively small caliber and light weight. Pulled along at a smart clip by teams of two to six sturdy farm horses, they could be swung quickly into position to shower the enemy lines with a deadly hail of grapeshot.

In the 1500's many classes of cannon had been developed, and

CIVIL WAR RAILROAD MORTAR.

men let their fancies run free when naming them. *Serpentine* (after the dreaded serpent), *falcon* (after the fierce hunting hawk), *basilisk* (the name of a mythical monster), and *culverin* (derived from a Latin word for "snake") were some of the better-known classifications. Some of these names lasted down into the early 1800's.

A more prosaic way of classifiying cannons was by the weight of the ball they fired, such as 4-pounder, 6-pounder, or 24-pounder. A 24-pounder was about the heaviest field piece an army could maneuver with, but guns for use on ships could be much heavier. Some of the guns on eighteenth-century English warships, for example, fired balls weighing 48 pounds. Siege guns could be even bigger. Some mortars used by the Union forces in the American Civil War fired a 200-pound projectile. During the nineteenth century most nations shifted to expressing calibers in inches or millimeters. The conservative British, however, still refer colloquially to cannons as "25-pounders" and so on, although the official designations have been in inches for many years.

Many of the early cannons fired balls of stone, as did the mangonels and other siege engines they replaced. For one thing, stone was much cheaper than metal, even considering the labor required to chip it into shape. For another, a stone cannonball was lighter than a metal one of the same size, so it put less of a stress on the breech of the gun when it was fired, and the danger of the gun's blowing up was less. As better cannons were made, iron came to be the material generally used for cannonballs, although Spain and some other countries still had a few stone throwers in service as late as 1800.

Long ago infantry soldiers were nicknamed "cannon fodder," since their principal function seemed to be to stand in line and be mowed down by the enemy's cannon.

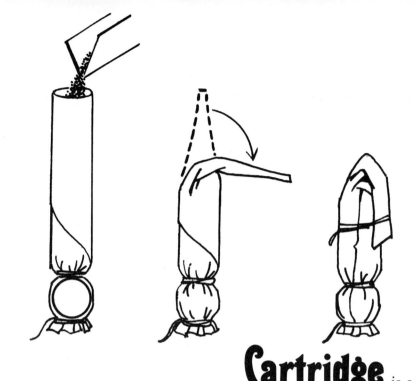

Cartridge is a

container that holds gunpowder and a bullet or shot. Modern cartridges also contain a primer, or explosive pellet that sets off the gunpowder.

The first known mention of cartridges was in the secret notebooks of Leonardo da Vinci, the famous artist and inventor, not long after 1500. But Leonardo wrote of them as something already well known.

The cartridges to which Leonardo referred were rolled-up tubes of paper containing a measured charge of gunpowder and sometimes a bullet as well. The word *cartridge* itself gives a clue to this origin, for it comes from *cartoccio,* an Italian term for a "paper scroll," which in turn comes from *carta,* an Italian word for "paper." In French this became *cartouche,* which went through some strange adaptations in English before taking on its present spelling, such as *cartage, cartruce,* and *cartrouche.*

To use a paper cartridge, you tore open one end, poured a little powder into the priming pan of your gun, and poured the rest down the barrel. Then you dropped the bullet in (it was little smaller than the inside of the gun barrel, so it dropped down easily) and rammed the paper down on top as a wad to hold everything in place.

Without the cartridge, you had to pour your powder from a powder horn, guessing at the right amount. If you used too much, the gun might explode in your face, perhaps blinding or killing you. If you used too little, the bullet would not have enough hitting power. Next, you had to fish a bullet out of a pouch that you wore on a belt called a *bandolier* slung over your shoulder. Then you had to get wadding from another pouch.

The cartridge not only guaranteed the correct load of powder, but also saved precious time in loading. To a soldier in the midst of a battle, this could spell the difference between life and death. During the second half of the 1500's, cartridges were used by cavalrymen. Early in the 1600's King Gustavus Adolphus of Sweden equipped his infantry soldiers with cartridges, greatly increasing their firepower. By the end of the century, cartridges were used by all the European armies.

Civilians, however, stuck pretty much to the old-fashioned method of loose powder and ball until the metal cartridge and the breech-loading gun came into general use in the 1860's. For one thing, hunters and target shooters liked to vary the charge of powder according to the distance from the target and the size of shot they were using. For another, cartridges were expensive. But mass production made metal cartridges cheap enough so that anyone could afford them. Today the only place you are likely to see anyone load a gun with loose powder and bullets is at a meeting of the National Muzzle-Loading Rifle Association.

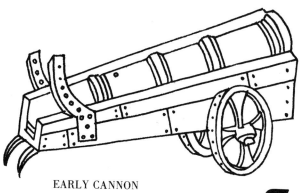

EARLY CANNON

firearm is

any weapon from which missiles are propelled by an explosion. This includes such large weapons as cannons and mortars, but in ordinary use it refers to weapons that can be carried by one person, such as rifles, shotguns, and pistols.

The word *firearm* dates from the 1600's, but a century earlier Frenchmen were talking about "firing" guns. In those days guns were literally "fired," since cannons were touched off by a burning length of fuze on the end of a pole, and hand weapons used either a fuze or a shower of sparks. Then, too, the black gunpowder that was then used went off with a bright muzzle flash and a big cloud of smoke.

The "smokeless" explosives used today make very little smoke and no flash that is visible in daylight. But *firearm* is still a technically accurate description, because an explosion is actually an extremely rapid burning.

The *arm* of *firearm* comes from a Latin word, *arma*, which referred to weapons or things used in fighting (See ARMS for details.) *Fire* comes from the Anglo-Saxon word *fyr*.

It is not known when the first firearms were invented, but primitive cannons were definitely being used in the early 1300's.

The knights and their hangers-on detested firearms, which took away some of the advantage they had up to then enjoyed over poorly armed infantry soldiers. (They also hated the crossbow and the longbow, which could wound or kill from a distance out of reach of the knight's sword.) The knightly class claimed that the gun was a coward's weapon and would spell the death of chivalry and bravery in battle. (They had previously said the same things about the bow.) Shakespeare, who lived in the last flickerings of the age of chivalry, expressed these feelings in a famous passage in his play *Henry IV* (Part I, Act I, Scene 3):

> And that it was great pity, so it was,
> This villanous salt-petre should be digg'd,
> Out of the bowels of the harmless earth,
> Which many a good tall fellow had destroy'd
> So cowardly. . . .

(Saltpeter was the principal ingredient of gunpowder.)

Despite sentiments like these, the knights themselves were not long in taking to firearms, often combined with a more traditional knightly weapon such as the mace or the battle-ax.

It has been said by many writers that firearms brought about the downfall of the feudal system. Actually, many factors were involved, but firearms were one of them. Cannons could batter down the stone walls of the stoutest castle, so the grim, fortified castles of the Middle Ages became useless. Deprived of their fortresses, the nobles lost a great deal of their independence and power, on which the feudal system was based. Furthermore, the development of the arquebus and the musket changed the character of war. Once the armored knight had been supreme on the battlefield—the medieval equivalent of a tank. But the musket made an unwarlike peasant the equal of the most martial knight.

ITALIAN SNAPHANCE
C. 1660

Flintlock was

a type of firearm in which the charge of powder was set off by sparks from a piece of flint striking against steel. Since ancient times it had been known that striking a piece of iron or steel against a chunk of flint would produce sparks that could start a fire. Sometime around the middle 1500's, someone thought of applying this familiar principle to guns.

Previously, guns had been fired by means of the matchlock, which used a burning wick called a *match* to set the powder off, or by the wheel lock, which worked somewhat like a giant cigarette lighter. Both these locks had their drawbacks, however. The matchlock would not work in rainy weather, and the wheel lock broke down too easily. Clearly, neither of them was the final answer to the shooter's problems.

The earliest type of flintlock was the snaphance, which was probably invented in the Netherlands some time before 1550.

Snaphance comes from the Dutch *snaphaan,* meaning "pecking rooster." Perhaps the action of the mechanism reminded people of a rooster pecking at its food.

The basic parts of the snaphance were a sharp-edged piece of flint; a cock, or movable holder for the flint; and a hinged steel plate over the priming pan for the flint to strike. The priming pan held a small charge of gunpowder which was set off by the sparks from the flint; a little hole led from the pan to the main charge of powder inside the barrel. The pan also had a sliding cover to protect the powder from the weather and keep it from spilling out. With the flint in place, the cock really did have some resemblance to the head and neck of a rooster, with the flint sticking out like a beak.

About the same time as the snaphance was invented, a similar lock called the *miquelet* was invented in Italy or Spain. The miquelet was like the snaphance in most respects, but it was a more rugged mechanism. The origin of the name is unknown, but romantic nineteenth-century writers theorized that it came from a gang of Spanish robbers called *Miqueletes,* or "Little Michaels." Supposedly the Miqueletes dared not run the risk of being detected by the glow of a burning matchlock match, but they could not afford wheel locks. Therefore, the talented criminals devised a snapping-action flintlock. This story may be characterized as picturesque hogwash. The Miquelete gangsters did indeed exist, but there is not the least evidence that they ever invented a gun lock. The Spaniards themselves called the lock a *patilla,* or "little foot."

The true flintlock, according to gun experts, was born when a French gunsmith combined features of the snaphance and the miquelet. Sturdy and reliable, it seems to have been invented between 1610 and 1615. It soon became the standard type of firing mechanism and lasted almost unchanged for more than 200

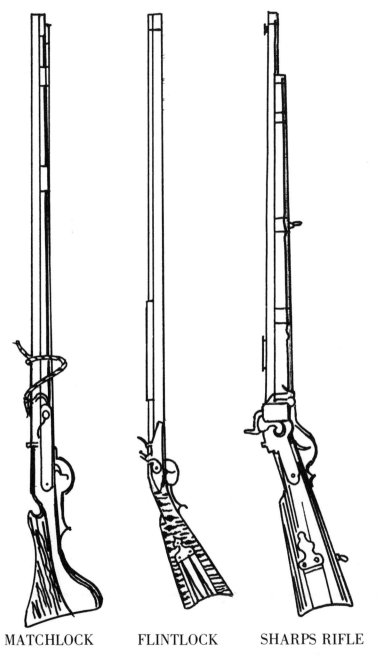

MATCHLOCK

SEVENTEENTH CENTURY

FLINTLOCK

C. 1790

SHARPS RIFLE

BREECHLOADER, C. 1840

years. Not until 1839, for example, did the British army drop the flintlock in favor of a more modern system. The United States army did not completely give up the flintlock until 1841. Even into the early years of the twentieth century, a few firms were busy making flintlocks for sale to African tribesmen.

Although the flintlock was invented early in the 1600's, it did not acquire its name until near the end of the century. Interestingly, in many European languages its name means either "flintlock" or something close to it. In French, for instance, it is *fusil à pierre*, or "stone gun," and in German *Steinschloss*, or "stone lock." In Spanish it is *llave de chispa*, or "lock of flint," and in Swedish it is *flintlås*, or "flintlock."

Some picturesque expressions have come from the flintlock. One is "going off half-cocked." The flintlock had a built-in safety feature: When the cock was pulled back halfway, a catch clicked into place and kept it from snapping forward if the trigger was pulled accidentally. The gun was then said to be "half-cocked." (It was "cocked" when the cock was pulled all the way back.) But when the parts of the lock became worn, it often happened that the catch no longer held properly, and the gun would go off half-cocked, sometimes causing an accident. From this, "going off half-cocked" came to be used to describe a person who acted impulsively before thinking things through.

"Flash in the pan" is another expression we owe to the flintlock. If the little hole that led from the pan to the powder in the gun barrel was not kept cleaned out, it became clogged with gummy residue from the burned powder, and the flame from the pan could not get through. When the shooter pulled his trigger, the powder in the pan flashed up into flame, just as it was supposed to do, but the gun would not fire. And so "flash in the pan" came to mean a brief, spectacular success followed by ignominious failure.

Grapeshot was

an early form of fragmentation weapon. It consisted of iron pellets an inch or two in diameter packed in bags. The appearance must have reminded gunners of a cluster of grapes, especially since the pellets were packed around a wooden rod, which may have suggested a stem. (The purpose of the rod, which was fastened to a wooden base disk, was to give shape to the bag of shot.)

Grapeshot was fired from cannons, and it was fearful in its effect. The bag burst as it left the cannon's muzzle, and the shot spread out in a wide canopy of death. Effective up to half a mile, it could mow down a whole line of troops. At sea, it could rip the sails and rigging of a ship to shreds and mangle any sailors unfortunate enough to get in the way. Grapeshot was used up to the early 1800's, when it was replaced by canister shot. This was similar to grapeshot, but it was packed in a metal canister like a cooky tin instead of in a bag. It was more effective at close range than grapeshot.

Grape comes from the French *grappe,* meaning "a bunch of grapes." Language scholars trace this word back to an old Germanic term for a kind of hook used in harvesting grapes. *Shot* comes from the verb *to shoot,* and its use to mean "a bullet" or "cannonball" goes back at least to the late 1400's. Put the two words together, and you get *grapeshot,* whose first recorded use was in 1747. Previously, it was simply called *grape.* Grapeshot was probably invented in the late 1500's, and it was definitely being used in the 1600's.

The phrase "a whiff of grapeshot" was once enshrined in nearly every history book that covered the French Revolution. In the fall of 1795, an enraged mob of Parisians threatened to attack the National Convention, one of the short-lived revolutionary governments that shakily attempted to rule France after the king was overthrown. The frightened government called out all the troops whose loyalty they could count on. Many of the soldiers were siding with the mob. The situation was grim.

In desperation, someone thought of offering command of the loyal troops to an ambitious young officer named Napoleon Bonaparte. Napoleon quickly sent a task force to seize the army's cannons and set them up in strategic places. The mob opened fire with their muskets and began to advance, but they were met by a hail of grapeshot from Napoleon's cannons. Within two hours the uprising was quelled. The grateful government later rewarded Napoleon with a high army post, and he was launched on his way to becoming Emperor of France.

The famous English writer Thomas Carlyle years later used the expression "a whiff of grapeshot" to describe the event, and other historians picked it up and used it as if it were their own.

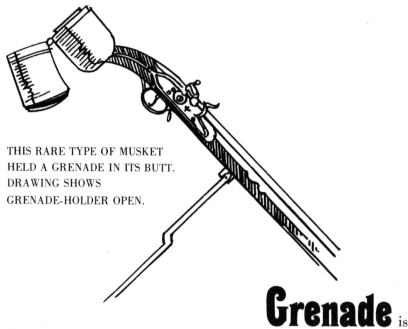

THIS RARE TYPE OF MUSKET
HELD A GRENADE IN ITS BUTT.
DRAWING SHOWS
GRENADE-HOLDER OPEN.

Grenade is

the French word for a "pomegranate," a kind of fruit. The pomegranate is filled with seeds; in fact, its original name in Latin, *pomum granatum*, means "a seedy apple."

Grenades were originally small, hollow metal shells filled with gunpowder. They were designed to explode and shower enemy troops with lethal chunks and slivers of metal. It is thought that grenades received their name because they were about the size and shape of a pomegranate or perhaps because they exploded like an overripe pomegranate hurled against a wall. Grenades were first used in the 1500's, and the name dates back to 1591.

Grenades were made both for shooting from a specially adapted musket and for throwing. Mostly, they were thrown. They proved so effective that in the late 1600's the French army began training specialists in the use of grenades. The English and other nations quickly followed suit.

The grenadiers, as the grenade throwers were termed, were always chosen from the biggest and strongest men in the army, since it required a good deal of strength to hurl a grenade far enough to reach the enemy and not hurt your own side. One of the grenadiers' special missions was assaulting forts. After softening up the enemy with a barrage of grenades, they would charge the fort and break open its massive wooden gates with axes.

In all the European armies, the grenadiers came to be looked on as elite troops. They were given distinctive, eye-catching uniforms, and they marched in the position of honor in parades. They wore special headgear, either a huge, furry cap of bearskin or a tall, pointed cap like a bishop's miter, often decorated with gleaming brass plates.

One of the most stirring military marches ever written was "The British Grenadier," which was a favorite marching song of British soldiers at the time of the American Revolution. It was so popular that the Americans turned it into a Revolutionary song by setting new words to it. (Nobody remembers the American version now, however, and you will find it only in very old collections of songs.)

Tactics eventually changed, and the grenadiers were no longer needed as bomb throwers. But Europe's kings were not about to give up their most impressive troops. Instead, they converted the grenadiers into royal palace guards, parade units, and elite infantry regiments.

Modern grenades are vastly improved over the original model, but no one writes songs about them. Fortunately, war seems to be losing some of its glamor. One nickname for the modern grenade is distinctly unglamorous: "pineapple." This nickname dates from World War I. By then grenades had been given an oval shape, and their sides were deeply scored with crisscross grooves to make sure they they broke up with maximum effect. To imaginative soldiers, their appearance suggested a pineapple.

In the same war, German troops used another type of grenade, which looked like a tin can on the end of a wooden handle. Allied troops were quick to dub this ungainly but effective weapon a "potato masher."

Gun as

most people use the word, covers any sort of firearm from a cannon to a .22-caliber pistol. *Gun* is also used for weapons that are not firearms at all, such as the air gun, which uses compressed air to propel its missiles, and the ray guns of science fiction. It is even used for tools whose general shape suggests a gun, such as the auto mechanic's grease gun and the carpenter's calking gun.

But in military usage *gun* always refers to a weapon too large to be fired from the hand or the shoulder, and career army men are very strict about the distinction. Cadremen (NCO's in charge of training recruits) used to take a sadistic delight in teaching new soldiers the difference. A luckless recruit who called his rifle a "gun" might be ordered to take it to bed with him. At the very least, he would be held up to ridicule in front of his whole platoon.

Gun was not the earliest name for a firearm, but it goes back before 1350. It was then written *gonne*. Historians' best guess is that it was a short form of Gunhilda, a woman's name often given as a nickname to big siege weapons such as catapults.

Another theory is that *gun* was someone's attempt to imitate the bellowing boom of an early cannon being fired.

Once it came into common use, *gun* gave rise to all sorts of derivatives, such as *gunpowder, gunner, gunsmith, gunwale,* and *gunman,* to name just a few.

In the early 1800's a "great gun" was one of the largest cannons a warship could carry. Thus, "great gun" came to be used for a very important person, or as we would say today, a "big gun." "To blow great guns" meant that the wind was making as much noise as a volley of shots from great guns, and "to go great guns" implied great energy and progress in doing a job.

Gunwale is the upper edge of a ship's or boat's side. It was formerly a heavy timber, or wale, that ran the length of the ship to hold the weight of the heavy guns; hence, *"gun-wale."* For hundreds of years, sailors have perversely insisted on pronouncing it "gunnel," to rhyme with *funnel.*

"To spike the guns" of someone means to render him powerless. This expression goes back to the days when cannons were fired by lighting a fuse in a touchhole. In a battle, picked assault troops would try to rush the enemy's guns and drive spikes into the touchholes, so that the guns could not be fired. The rest of the army could then advance without having to face grapeshot or cannonballs. Sometimes a retreating army, forced to leave its guns behind, would spike them to keep the foe from using them.

But sometimes the gunners refused to abandon their cannon, no matter how great their danger. They remained at their posts and kept on fighting. From this comes the expression "to stick to one's guns," meaning to stand by a position you have taken.

"To gun an engine" means to apply full power. Presumably this expression comes from the roar that a gasoline engine makes when running wide open.

Gunpowder,

according to a popular Medieval legend, was invented by a wicked German monk, Schwarze Berthold (Black Berthold), with the aid of the devil. One of the tale's many versions is that Black Berthold was a practitioner of alchemy and black magic. While trying to find a way to create gold, he put mercury, sulfur, and saltpeter into a caldron and set it on a hot fire. As he waited with greedy anticipation for the mixture to turn into gold, it exploded with a roar, hurling the lid of the caldron through the stone ceiling of his monastic cell. Sniggering with evil delight at the destruction he had created, Berthold picked himself up and went on to invent the gun as well.

There is no proof that Black Berthold ever really existed, but historians picked up the tale and treated it as true, and you can still find it in books. A good story dies hard.

A less fanciful theory is that gunpowder was invented by Roger Bacon, an English monk who lived from about 1214 to about 1294. Bacon was a real man and one of the finest scholars of his time. One of his code writings describes gunpowder and gives a workable formula for making it, but modern scholars believe that he had learned about it in the writings of other experimenters. Bacon may have done experiments with gunpowder but, as far as is known, never considered using it to hurl a projectile through the air.

The Chinese used gunpowder to propel arrows. They were launched from decorated boxes, like this one, and powered by a powder-filled capsule attached to the shaft.

The first people to make gunpowder were the Chinese, who were probably using it in firecrackers as early as the 1100's. By the 1200's they were definitely using it to make explosive bombs and a crude kind of military rocket, which they used against the Mongol invaders of China. The Chinese did not invent guns, however. This questionable blessing reached them from the West.

Arab traders may have carried the secret of gunpowder from China to the Middle East, or Arab and Byzantine alchemists may have invented it independently in the 1200's. At any rate, by the early 1300's it was well known not only in the Arab lands, but also in Europe, and primitive guns were being used by the 1320's. The word *gunpowder* itself dates from the 1300's, probably the later part of the century.

The original gunpowder, or black powder, was made from saltpeter, charcoal, and sulfur, all ground up fine and mixed together. Since at first there was no standard formula for gunpowder, the proportions of each ingredient varied a good deal, and so did the strength of the powder. An early gunner was never quite sure whether his cannonball would shoot out powerfully or plop weakly to the ground a few feet beyond the muzzle of the gun—or even if the powder would go off at all. Sometimes the powder was stronger than expected, and the gun would blow up. All in all, it was a chancy business.

When barrels of gunpowder were carted to the battlefield or siege place, the ingredients tended to separate out into different layers. Then the whole barrelful had to be mixed over again. Sometimes gunners would have a barrel of each ingredient and mix their own powder on the spot as they needed it.

Early in the 1400's the process of corning powder was discovered. The powdered saltpeter, charcoal, and sulfur were mixed as before, but then they were moistened with water to make a pasty mush that was forced through a sieve. The long strings of powder mixture that came out of the sieve were cut into grains, or corns (*corn* originally meant "grain" or "seed"), and then dried. Corned powder did not come unmixed in a jolting cart, and in addition, the grains could be made in standard sizes, so that the rate of burning and the strength of the explosion could be controlled.

Black powder was not foolproof, however, even when corned. Aside from the danger of accidental explosions, when it got damp it would not fire. And it soaked up moisture from the air with distressing ease. Damp powder was one of the nightmares of the soldier.

From a fairly early date, soldiers carried their powder in paper cartridges that contained a measured charge. But hunters carried their powder loose in a container. Well-to-do men sported a decorative brass powder flask, but poorer folk discovered that a cow's horn would do as well. The big end of the horn had a lid with a hole in it for filling the horn; the tip was cut off to make a spout for pouring powder into the gun. Both holes were plugged up when not in use. The powder horn, whose name goes back to the 1530's, was used well into the 1800's.

"Remember, remember the fifth of November, the Gunpowder Treason and Plot! I see no reason why Gunpowder Treason should ever be forgot!" So goes an English folk rhyme that commemorates one of the most sensational episodes in England's history, the Gunpowder Plot.

In 1605, England had been Protestant for nearly half a century, though many people still adhered to the old Roman Catholic faith. Feeling was bitter between the two faiths. A small group of Catholic fanatics convinced each other that the time was ripe to seize control of England for Catholicism again, and they made plans to blow up Parliament when the king addressed it. This would get rid of not only the king, but many other important leaders as well.

The conspirators managed to smuggle more than a ton and a half of gunpowder into the cellar of the House of Lords, hiding it under loads of coal and firewood. All was set to touch off the powder when the king addressed Parliament on November 5.

But a few days before the fateful date one of the conspirators warned a friend not to attend Parliament. The friend, in turn, alerted the king's ministers. On the night of November 4 the cellar was searched, and a plotter named Guy Fawkes was caught guarding the gunpowder. Fawkes was arrested and tortured to make him reveal the names of his fellow conspirators. All of them who were taken alive were tried for treason and executed.

Fawkes was not the leader of the conspiracy or even one of the original members. But since he was the one who had been caught with the gunpowder, the public imagination turned him into the most important person in the plot, and November 5 came to be called Guy Fawkes Day. It was celebrated by setting off firecrackers and burning straw effigies of the detested Fawkes. These straw men, called *Guys* after the man they represented, were dressed in grotesque costumes and carried through the streets until evening, when they were given their fiery sendoff. In time, *guy* became a slangy synonym for a grotesque or eccentric man. Around the end of the 1800's, Americans were using *guy* to mean simply "man" or "boy," as they do today. And Guy Fawkes Day is still celebrated in England.

Lock, Stock, and Barrel were

the main parts of a gun for about 400 years. The lock was the mechanism that set off the gunpowder. The barrel was the tube-like part of the gun down which bullets, pellets, and other projectiles traveled. The stock was the wooden part of the gun to which the barrel and the lock were fastened. Modern guns have barrels and stocks, but not locks.

Locks, stocks, and barrels were often made by different craftsmen. A gunsmith might make his own barrel, buy the lock and the stock from other specialists, put them together, and sell the gun under his own name. "Lock, stock, and barrel" was the phrase used by buyers and sellers to specify a complete gun. Later it lost its original meaning and came to be no more than a colorful way of saying "everything." For example, one might say, "When old Mr. Morgan retired, he handed his whole business over to his son-in-law, lock, stock, and barrel."

Historically, the first of the trio to appear was the barrel. The earliest guns were cannons, and they were nothing but tubes to contain powder and projectiles. While gunmakers could cast small cannon barrels, they had no way of casting big ones. Instead, the gunmaker and his workmen would take a load of long, broad iron bars called *staves*, heat them red-hot, and hammer them together lengthwise, edge to edge, to form a tube. This primitive welding process was done over a big, round wooden core that gave the tube more or less the right size and shape.

But this tube of welded metal strips was not strong enough to withstand the force of an exploding charge of gunpowder, not even the weak black powder of the 1300's. To reinforce the tube, the gunmakers slid a series of heated iron hoops down over it, one after the other, until they covered the entire length of the tube. As the hoops cooled off, they shrank, holding the lengthwise bars tightly together, just as a barrelmaker used iron hoops to hold the wooden staves of his barrels. Because of this similarity between barrelmaking and gunmaking, Englishmen called the tube of a gun the *barrel*, and the name stuck.

Sixteenth Century ship's cannon
shows hoop and stave construction.

The stock came in with the invention of handguns—that is, guns small enough to be carried and used by one man. The word *stock* comes from the Anglo-Saxon word *stoc*, meaning the "stem or trunk of a tree." The earliest handguns, made around 1350, were fastened on the ends of wooden poles—the first stocks. The shooter held the pole just behind the gun barrel with one hand and clamped the pole tightly under his arm. With the other hand, he pressed a glowing coal (held in tongs) to the touchhole of the gun. Needless to say, it was impossible to aim a gun like this accurately.

As gun design improved, gunmakers began to fasten the barrel on top of the stock instead of on the end. The stock was hollowed out lengthwise to form a cradle for the barrel, which was held in place by iron bands. The shooter held the end of the stock on top of his shoulder, next to his cheek. This improved his aim, since he could now sight down the barrel. But he had to absorb the "kick" with his wrists and arms, which must have caused many sprains.

Spanish gunmakers of the 1500's finally solved this problem. They broadened the end of the stock so that it could rest against the shooter's shoulder, as in a modern gun. The shooter could

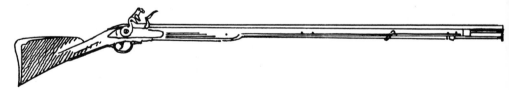

BRITISH INFANTRY MUSKET

now hold his weapon firmly and aim it more accurately. And even the strongest man found that his shoulder could take the recoil of a gun much better than his wrists and arms. The sixteenth-century Spanish design has not changed, except in details, down to the present day.

The lock was the last part of the gun to be invented. It was the most difficult part to make, because a lock was composed of a number of small parts that had to fit together just right; otherwise, the lock would jam and the gun would be useless. Lacking machines for shaping metal, lockmakers had to forge each piece by hand to more or less the right dimensions, then finish it off by the tedious process of hand filing. There was no such thing as standardization. No two workmen ever made parts quite the same. You could not take a spare part from the lock of another gun and use it to fix your own lock, because it would be just a little too big here or a little too small there. Not until Eli Whitney created a system of fixtures to guide workmen's tools could standard, interchangeable parts be manufactured. And this was not until the end of the 1700's.

There were four types of lock. The oldest was the matchlock, which used a burning piece of wick called a *match* to set off the powder. Next came the wheel lock, in which a revolving wheel created a shower of sparks to ignite the powder. This was replaced by the flintlock, in which a piece of flint struck against a steel plate to produce sparks. Last of all came the percussion lock, in which a tiny charge of explosive chemicals was exploded by a blow from a hammer. Each of these locks is described in detail in a separate entry.

The word *lock* can be traced back to an Old Germanic root, *luk*, meaning "to close." It has been applied to guns since about 1550, but how and why it came to be used in connection with firearms we do not know.

𝕸atchlock was

a very early type of gun in which the powder was ignited by a
piece of slow-burning wick called a *match*.

The first handguns—miniature cannons on the end of a stout
pole—had to be fired by pressing a red-hot iron or a glowing
coal to the touchhole. This was not only difficult and dangerous
to the gunner, but it also meant that he could never go far from

a fire to keep him supplied with heat. Then came the match, a length of loosely woven cord soaked in saltpeter and then dried. The saltpeter helped the match to burn slowly and evenly. When one end of the match was lit, it would smolder away until the match was burned up. A long match might be good for several hours. With a match to touch off his gun, the gunner could move freely about; he did not risk severe burns on his hands, as he did with the glowing coal; and he could easily light a new match from the glowing stub of the old one.

The next improvement was a holder for the match. This was a metal lever shaped somewhat like a Z with a long-drawn-out tail. It was pivoted to the stock through its crossbar, and the lighted match was clamped in the short arm of the Z. Moving the long arm lowered the match to the touchhole. The shape and motion of the lever suggested a striking snake, and so it was called a *serpentine.*

The true matchlock was born about 1475, when someone modified the design and added a spring to push the serpentine away from the powder, which by now lay in a small pan, the priming pan, on the side of the gun. To fire the gun, you pressed a trigger, which overcame the slight force of the spring and gently lowered the match onto the powder in the pan. The moving parts of the mechanism were placed inside the stock, out of harm's way, and further protected by a metal plate.

About the same time, a snapping matchlock was invented. In this type of gun, a spring snapped the match down onto the pan when the shooter pressed a button. However, the force of the match snapping down often scattered the powder or put out the match instead of firing the gun, so it was not a success.

The matchlock was far from an ideal weapon. It was slow to load and to fire. There was always a lag of a second or two between the time the shooter lowered the match to the pan and the

time the bullet left the muzzle of the gun. During that time, the
target might have moved away. Worse yet, it would fire only
under favorable conditions. The match could be extinguished by
a high wind, rain, or even a heavy fog. Then the gun was good
only for a club. Also, at night the glow of the match could give
away your position to your enemies.

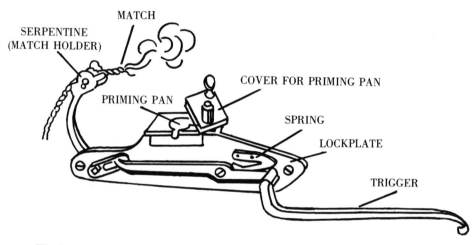

Working parts of a matchlock—

Better weapons—the wheel lock and the ancestors of the flintlock—were invented in the 1500's. But the matchlock was
cheaper to make and easier to repair. And so, in spite of its
inefficiency, the matchlock remained the standard gun for European foot soldiers until about 1700, when the flintlock was generally adopted.

Match goes back to the days when lamps were shaped like gravy boats, with a handle at one end and a nozzle at the other. The nozzle held a wick that dipped down into the vegetable oil with which the lamp was filled. The Romans called this lamp nozzle a *myxa*. In the later days of the Roman Empire, *myxa* became *micca*, and now it meant the wick itself. As French developed out of Latin, the word became *meiche*, still signifying a wick. The Norman conquest brought *meiche* to England, where the famed English dislike of foreign pronunciations turned it into *match* sometime before 1400.

Matchlock is a much later word, however. It did not appear in English until just before 1700. By then the wheel lock and the flintlock had become so common in civilian use that it was necessary to distinguish the three types of lock.

In the early 1500's, the name *match* was also given to a fire-lighting device—a splinter of wood, a cord, or a strip of paper whose end had been dipped in sulfur. These could be lit very easily with a spark from flint and steel and then used for lighting fires, candles, or what-have-you. When the self-lighting "lucifer match" was invented in 1831, the title of *match* was naturally applied to it. Today's safety matches bear the same name as a token of their descent from that ancient lighting device, the Roman lampwick.

Musket was

a smoothbore shoulder gun that fired a heavy lead ball. The
name is believed to come from *moschetto*, the Italian name for
the "sparrowhawk." *Moschetto* may in turn be derived from
mosca, the Italian word for "fly." Perhaps this was because of
the sparrowhawk's small size or perhaps because it eats flies
when nothing better is available. Since men of the Renaissance
had a fondness for naming weapons after predatory birds and
beasts, the musket was given the name of this fierce little hawk.

Another theory is that *musket* comes from a very similar
Italian word, *moschetta*, the name of a crossbow missile. Perhaps

the crossbow missile buzzed in flight like a gigantic fly and stung when it landed. At this date, it is hard to know.

When the musket first appeared, probably about 1535, it was a very large, heavy weapon. Its long, thick-walled barrel had a caliber of 10 or even 8 bore (.778 or .80 inch). The whole musket was as tall as a man and weighed about 20 pounds. No one could hold a monster like this steady on a target, so the musket had to be fired from a crutchlike support.

Despite its size and awkwardness, the musket was an effective weapon. Its massive ball, weighing up to $\frac{1}{8}$ pound, could crash through any armor light enough to wear. This had a good deal to do with the disappearance of armor.

The musket was a Spanish invention, and it was used by the Spanish armies in the Netherlands when the Dutch were fighting Spain for their independence and religious freedom in the middle 1500's. Observers from other nations were quick to note the musket's effectiveness, and their armies were quick to adopt the new gun. The Spaniards called the gun *mosquete*, and the French *mousquet*. In fact, the name was remarkably similar all over Europe. The musket was apparently being used in England by the 1560's, although the first recorded use of the name was in 1587.

Over the years, the musket was gradually made smaller and lighter, until it no longer needed to be fired from a support. (The large caliber remained about the same, however.) By the mid-1600's there was no longer any real difference between the musket, the arquebus, and other long-barreled shoulder guns. Eventually, musket became the general term for all smoothbore shoulder guns.

"Brown Bess" was the nickname of one famous type of musket. This was the flintlock musket issued to British troops in the early 1700's and used for well over a century. The nickname may have

come from the fact that the barrels of these muskets were treated to give them a rust-resistant brown finish that would not glare in the sun and blind the soldiers. Many British soldiers, however, felt that the dull, brown finish spoiled their fine appearance on parade; so they proceeded to polish off the browning until their musket barrels gleamed like silver. Few soldiers in any modern army would follow their example.

Muskets were the chief weapon of both sides during the American Revolution. The British carried the .75-caliber Brown Bess, while the Americans were mostly equipped with the .69-caliber French Charleville musket, an equally good weapon. A generation later, Napoleon's soldiers conquered most of Europe with the Charleville musket. In fact, armies did not switch completely from muskets to rifles until the 1840's and 1850's.

At one time, musketeers were an elite corps. In the 1600's, King Louis XIII of France maintained a picked group of musketeers for his palace guard. One of the most famous novels ever published, *The Three Musketeers*, was written about these guardsmen and their adventures. Completed in 1844, it was translated into many languages and was an instant best seller. It was also dramatized as a play and in modern times was made into several movie versions. The book, a romantic tale filled with suspense, danger, and intrigue and based on real events, is still popular.

The original three musketeers, Àthos, Porthos, and Aramis, and their friend D'Artagnan were actual people, and the novel was based in large part on D'Artagnan's memoirs. After a bad beginning, in which he is forced to accept challenges to duels with the three musketeers all on the same day, D'Artagnan and the three companions become devoted friends and allies. Thanks to the novel's popularity, "three musketeers" became a synonym for very close friends.

Muzzle-loader and Breechloader were

two different types of gun. In the early days of gunnery, men fancifully named the front end of a gun barrel its *mouth* or *muzzle*, as if the gun were a living creature. It is not hard to see why. This was the end through which the gun "spoke" and through which it "spit" its deadly load. Following the same line of reasoning, the other end of the gun barrel was named the *breech*, from an old word referring to the rear end of a person or animal.

Muzzle comes from the Old French word *musel*, meaning the "snout or mouth of an animal." *Breech* comes from an Anglo-Saxon word, *brec*, which was originally the name of a garment something like a pair of knee-length shorts. (Our modern word *breeches* comes from the same root.) Later, *breech* came to mean the part of the body covered by this garment, particularly the buttocks, or "rear end."

EARLY BREECHLOADER CANNON

A muzzle-loader was a gun that was loaded by way of the muzzle. To accomplish this, you had to pour your gunpowder down the barrel, drop in a bullet, and then stuff a bunch of wadding into the muzzle. Then you had to tamp the whole collection down with your ramrod. This was a clumsy and time-consuming procedure, and men realized quite early how much easier it would be to have a breech that could be opened up to put in the load.

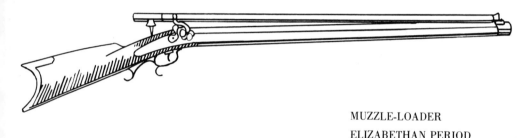

MUZZLE-LOADER
ELIZABETHAN PERIOD

Yet, down to about 1860, the vast majority of the guns in the world were muzzle-loaders, for the very good reason that early gunsmiths had been unable to make a breechloader that didn't leak at the breech when the gun was fired. A cloud of smoke, flame, and scalding gases a few inches from your face was unpleasant at best, and it could cause serious injury. A leaky breech also wasted some of the force of the exploding gunpowder.

Breech-loading cannons were made in the early 1400's, and

breech-loading pistols and shoulder guns were made at least as early as 1537. However, the problem of leakage kept them from general use. Even the best-made breechloaders tended to leak as their parts wore down under use.

A really satisfactory breechloader was not made until the time of the American Revolution, and even so breechloaders were uncommon for another half century, until most of the technical problems had been overcome.

Military leaders were slow to accept the breechloader, and not merely because of the tradition-bound official's dislike of anything new. One reason advanced for not buying breechloaders for the troops was, indeed, rather foolish: that soldiers would fire too many shots a minute, thus using up excessive quantities of powder and lead. But there were more valid reasons. For one thing, early breechloaders tended to foul after a few shots— that is, the gummy residue of the burned powder would cake up, jamming the breech mechanism. Again, breechloaders were more expensive than muzzle-loaders, since they needed more parts and those parts had to be accurately made. Then, too, early breech-loaders were not rugged. They needed careful handling, which was not to be expected from the ordinary soldier. Not until all these weaknesses had been overcome and troops armed with breechloaders had shot rings around enemies armed with muzzle-loaders in actual battles did the army officials give in. After breechloaders had proved their effectiveness in the American Civil War, they were adopted by all the major armies.

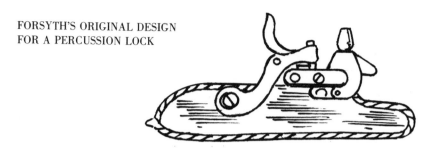

Percussion Lock was

the last type of lock to be used before the invention of the self-contained cartridge made locks unnecessary. It used an explosive chemical compound to set off the charge of powder in the gun.

By the end of the 1700's the young science of chemistry had made tremendous advances, and chemists were continually producing startling new substances. Among these were a group of highly sensitive explosive compounds called *fulminates* (from the Latin *fulmen,* meaning a "lightning bolt" or a "thunderclap"). If a little fulminate powder were poured out on a table and tapped lightly, it would explode with a violent bang.

A young Scottish minister and chemistry hobbyist named Alexander Forsyth thought that perhaps a tiny charge of fulminate could be used to set off gunpowder. In 1805, after several years of trial and failure, he finally found a way to do so.

The new invention received the name of *percussion system,* because the fulminate was set off by the blow of a hammer, rather than by a spark from flint and steel. *Percussion,* by the way, comes from the Latin *percussio,* "a sharp blow."

Forsyth's percussion lock, although ingenious, had a number of problems, as is apt to happen with original inventions. A number of other men worked out improved systems, but in the end one system came into almost universal use.

136

This system, invented around 1815, used a dab of fulminate compound about the size of a match head inside a little, thimble-shaped metal cap. The cap was placed on top of a hollow steel nipple that led directly into the breech cavity of the gun. When the trigger was pulled, a hammer struck the cap, setting off the fulminate, which in turn set off the gunpowder.

The percussion lock was much more reliable than the flintlock, and it did not have the flintlock's slight lag between the pull on the trigger and the actual discharge of the gun. It would fire even in a rainstorm. It had fewer parts than the flintlock, thus fewer parts to get lost or broken. And it misfired less frequently.

Civilians soon took to the percussion system. Armies were slower to make the switch. For one thing, they all had large supplies of flintlocks in perfectly good condition, and they did not want to junk these guns. For another, they did not want to adopt a new system until all the "bugs" had been worked out. And for some reason a percussion gun shot a bit less hard than a flintlock with an identical load.

Therefore the changeover was gradual. The United States army, for instance, began issuing limited numbers of percussion guns in 1833, but they were not made standard for all troops until 1842. France began issuing percussion guns in 1829 and finished the job in 1840. Britain, Switzerland, and Austria-Hungary also went all percussion in 1842.

But the percussion system was not destined to have a long career. The self-contained, metal based cartridge, which contained its own primer, was on its way. It was this cartridge that made the breech-loading gun fully practical. Shortly after the American Civil War, the world's major armies switched to breech-loading guns using the new cartridge. The era of modern firearms had begun.

Pistol is

a small firearm held in one hand of the shooter. The name is most probably derived from the northern Italian city of Pistoia, where the first pistols may have been made. The *Oxford English Dictionary* traces *pistol* back to *pistolese*, the Italian adjective for people or things from Pistoia. *Pistolese* would thus be the name for a Pistoian weapon. (Interestingly enough, *pistolese* was also the name of a kind of large dagger, and *dagg*, an old English name for a dagger, was also used for an early type of pistol. Could there have been some connection in people's minds between different types of hand weapons?)

The French picked up *pistolese* from the Italians—French armies were campaigning in northern Italy around the time when pistols first appeared—and turned it into *pistolet*, later shortening it to *pistole*. After the mid-1500's the name crossed the Channel to England, where it lost its final *e*.

Some scholars believe that *pistol* is derived from the Czech

word *pistala*, meaning a "metal pipe or tube," and came to
French by way of the German version, *Pistole*. A short gun called
a *pistala*—a kind of sawed-off arquebus—was indeed used by the
Czechs in the 1400's. But the argument is one that can never
really be settled, since conclusive evidence for either side is
missing.

Wherever pistols were invented and whatever the origin of
their name may be, it is known that they were being made in
northern Italy in the early 1500's and that the authorities of
many cities tried unsuccessfully to ban them. Not only did the
easily concealed pistol lend itself to robbers, but ordinary
citizens were using them to settle their personal quarrels.

The pistol was invented at about the same time as the wheel
lock, and the great popularity of pistols was due to the wheel
lock. It would have been highly inconvenient to carry a gun with
a length of burning match stuck in your belt or in your pocket,

but the wheel lock avoided this difficulty. And so all but a very few of the early pistols were equipped with wheel locks.

For many years pistols bore little resemblance to their modern descendants. Instead of the familiar short, curved butt, they had a long, straight stock that made only a slight angle with the barrel. Often the stock ended in a heavy knob, which made a splendid club after the pistol's single shot had been fired.

A typical pistol of the 1500's measured some 2 feet overall, but it was still much easier to shoot and to carry than a 5-foot arquebus or a 6-foot musket. Its handiness made it a favorite cavalry weapon, and German mercenary cavalrymen employed by Henry VIII were using it in England as early as 1530. (The English did not use the word *pistol* until about 1570, however.) Henry, an enthusiastic collector of weapons, himself acquired a huge arsenal of pistols.

Cavalry pistols were too big and heavy to wear on one's person, so they were carried in holsters on the saddle. Because of this, they were often known as *horse pistols*.

Because the wheel lock was expensive to make, pistols were the weapons of people with plenty of money to spend. As a result, they were often elaborately and beautifully decorated. Such a pistol was as much a showpiece as a weapon. It might be engraved with scenes from classical mythology or inlaid with ivory and precious metals.

During the 1600's, pistol butts gradually took on a curved shape, and small, pocket-sized models were made. The flintlock took the place of the wheel lock, and pistols became more utilitarian. One problem with the pistol had always been that it fired only a single shot. This left the user vulnerable until he could reload it. To overcome this disadvantage, some people carried two or more pistols, while others used double-barreled pistols. Primitive revolvers were made as early as the 1500's, but they never worked very well. The first really satisfactory revolver was patented by Samuel Colt in 1834.

In the 1500's a mania for dueling seized France and soon spread from that center of fashion all over Europe. For a century or more, the "gentleman's" weapon of choice was the sword, but about 1650 firearms became popular dueling weapons. Although any weapon acceptable to both parties could be used, tradition and etiquette prescribed the pistol. Dueling pistols were beautifully made and very accurate. They were usually made in pairs so that both the challenger and the challengee would be equally armed.

Duels were fought for the most trifling of reasons. Men of that time had a very touchy and childish sense of honor and felt that the slightest "insult" had to be wiped out in blood. Furthermore, to refuse a challenge was to declare yourself a coward publicly, and few men cared to face that disgrace. Dueling did not really wane in popularity until the early 1800's, when public opinion changed.

One famous American duel was fought between Alexander Hamilton and Aaron Burr in 1804. Hamilton, who had not wanted the fight, fired his pistol into the ground. Burr took careful aim and inflicted a mortal wound on Hamilton. Both men were leading politicians and heroes of the Revolutionary War, and the public was so shocked by the outcome of their quarrel that dueling quickly became unpopular in the Northern states. In the South, however, it remained a popular recreation up to the Civil War.

In Shakespeare's time, *pistol* was an epithet for a swaggering bully. In fact, Shakespeare used the name Pistol for a comical ruffian who appeared in three of his plays. A "pocket pistol" was not only a weapon, but a little flask of liquor, just the right size to slip into one's pocket and sip an occasional "shot" from.

Ramrod was

a wooden or metal rod used to tamp down the load of powder and ball in a muzzle-loading firearm. If this were not done, the loose powder might give a weak explosion or might fail to go off at all. Early rifles needed especially strong ramrods, because the ball fitted the barrel very tightly and had to be hammered down.

After the Civil War, when breech-loading rifles came into general use, the ramrod was no longer needed for loading. However, for years military rifles were made with ramrods that served as cleaning rods and could also be used if necessary to push a stuck cartridge out of the breech of the gun.

Although ramrods were used from the earliest days of firearms, the English word *ramrod* was not used until the late 1700's. Before then it was simply called a *rammer.*

The *ram* portion of *ramrod* comes from the Middle English verb *rammen,* which originally meant "to pound loose earth with a heavy implement to make it hard and firm," as in making a dirt floor. *Rammen* later took on other meanings, such as "hammering down a post" or "tamping down a load of gunpowder." *Rammen* came from the Old English word *ramm,* "a male sheep," and probably refers to the ram's aggressive habit of butting.

Rod comes from the Old English *rodd,* which may be related to an Old Norse word meaning "club." *Rod* always carries the idea of an object that is slender for its size.

In days gone by, people would say of a very stiff, unfriendly person, "He acts as if he had a ramrod up his spine." The same description was applied to excessively strict military officers. On the other hand, "ramrod-straight" was a complimentary term, implying manly self-respect and independence.

In the Old West, *ramrod* meant a boss, foreman, or anyone else in authority. It was probably a cowboy's term, although some students of Western lore think that it originated in the logging camps. It was even used as a verb. "I ramrod this spread" meant "I'm the boss of this ranch," although this was probably heard more often in magazine stories than in real life.

Rifle in

its broadest sense, is any firearm that has spiral grooves on the inside of its barrel. But in everyday use it refers to a gun that is fired from the shoulder, excluding cannons and pistols. (Short, lightweight rifles are often called *carbines*.) The purpose of the grooves is to make the bullet spin as it travels through the air. This increases its accuracy.

Rifle probably comes from the French word *rifler*, meaning "to scratch" or "to scrape," referring to the grooves cut into the bore of a rifle. In the early days of riflemaking, these grooves were literally scraped into the soft iron of the barrel, a tiny fraction of an inch at a time, by a revolving cutter that was

pulled through the bore by hand. *Rifle* originally meant the grooves themselves; later it came to mean a gun that had a rifled barrel. Today the grooves are often referred to as *rifling*. The portions between the grooves are called *lands*.

The first rifles seem to have been made in southern Germany or Switzerland, probably a little before 1500. By 1550, at any rate, rifles were well known, although they were not common.

The spinning missile was not a new idea. Years before the rifle was invented, men had been setting the feathers of crossbow bolts and longbow arrows at an angle to give them a spin. They knew from experience, although they did not understand why, that a spinning missile flew straighter. This principle was later applied to firearms, resulting in the rifle.

In the early days of the rifle, a popular theory was that the spinning ball flew straighter because demons could not sit on it and spoil the aim. A countertheory was that demons so enjoyed the sensation of spinning around that they were almost certain to hop aboard a rifle ball and pilot it toward its target. Today we know that the mysterious something that keeps a rifle bullet on course is the same principle that keeps a spinning gyroscope steady.

At first, loading a rifle was a real test of strength. To get a proper spin, the ball had to fit tightly into the grooves, so it was made a hairsbreadth larger than the barrel. This meant that it had to be hammered all the way down. If the grooves of the rifling were fouled with burned powder, the job was well-nigh impossible. Sometimes the ramrod would break under this mistreatment.

About 1600 a better system was found. The ball was made slightly smaller than the barrel and wrapped in a greased patch of cloth or very thin leather. The patch assured a tight fit, yet it allowed the ball to be pushed down the barrel with much less effort. It also made a gas-tight seal between the ball and the barrel, and it helped keep the rifling clean. However, even with this improvement, it took a full minute to load a rifle, whereas a man with a smoothbore musket could get off three or four shots in that time. This kept the rifle from being very useful on the battlefield, although some European governments began equipping specially trained sharpshooters with rifles in the early 1600's. The main use of rifles was in hunting.

One well-known type of hunting rifle was the Kentucky rifle, which was actually developed by Swiss and German settlers in Pennsylvania around 1725. The part of Pennsylvania where these settlers lived was then a wild frontier, and they had a great need for accurate weapons. For one thing, they depended on hunting for a good deal of their food, and a good shot at a deer might mean the difference between starvation and survival. For another, there was always the danger of a raid by unfriendly Indians.

The European rifle that these Pennsylvania settlers were used to was a dumpy weapon with a short, wide barrel of .70 to .75 caliber and a huge butt. It was an accurate weapon, but it used a great deal of powder and lead, and these were hard to come by on the frontier. To save lead, the frontier gunmakers cut the caliber down to about .45. The smaller bullet, in turn, needed less powder to propel it. To make sure that all the powder burned and was not wasted, they lengthened the barrel to about $3\frac{1}{2}$ feet. They found that this gun, with its smaller caliber, did not have nearly the "kick" of the European rifle, and so they were able to make the butt slender and graceful. This was the gun made famous by men like Daniel Boone and Daniel Morgan, and almost every frontiersman made it his business to own one.

The Kentucky rifle was originally called simply the *long rifle* or the *American rifle*. But in the Battle of New Orleans, in 1814, Andrew Jackson's Kentucky volunteers, armed with the backwoodsman's long rifle, won such a decisive victory over the British that a hero-worshiping public named it the *Kentucky rifle.*

Slow loading was the rifle's main defect, and for years men had been trying to cure this by making the rifle a breechloader. The early experiments were not successful, mainly because it was too difficult to keep a blast of burning gas from leaking out through the joints of the breech mechanism. The first really practical breech-loading rifle was perfected in 1776 by a British army officer, Patrick Ferguson. It had a breech that screwed open and closed. But Ferguson was killed in the Revolutionary War, and his rifle was never given a real chance.

During the last years of the 1700's and the early 1800's, ideas for breechloaders sprang up like weeds. There were screw-type breeches. There were hinged barrels that swung down to open up the breech. There were hinged breechblocks that tilted up for easy loading. There were falling blocks and rolling blocks. A number of these designs were adopted by armies for a limited number of troops, on an experimental basis.

HALL RIFLE,
BREECHLOADER OPEN

Then came an invention that gave the muzzle-loader a new lease on life. This was a cone-shaped bullet with a hollow base. The bullet fit the barrel loosely, so that it could be rammed home with a single easy stroke. When the rifle was fired, the explosion expanded the base of the bullet and made it grip the rifling tightly. This expanding-base bullet was generally known as the minié *ball*, after a French army captain, Claude Étienne Minié, who had carried out a series of experiments with it. (Actually it had been invented by another French army captain, Gustave Delvigne, but for some reason Minié got the credit for it.) Muzzle-loading rifles using minié balls were the most common weapons on both sides during the American Civil War. They were given the odd name of *rifle-musket*, apparently because they had long barrels like the muskets they replaced, while the earlier army rifles had short barrels.

During the Civil War it was noticed that troops armed with breech-loading rifles could fire much faster than those shooting muzzle-loaders. In some cases, soldiers were so anxious to get breechloaders that they purchased them with their own money when the government would not supply them. Convinced by the results, the world's armies changed over to breechloaders.

Repeating rifles also had their tryout in the Civil War and passed with flying colors. One make of repeater, the Winchester, became as much a part of the Westerner's "survival kit" as his Colt revolver. However, repeaters were not adopted for army use for about twenty more years. As with earlier innovations, army chiefs of staff were very cautious.

Finally Germany, driven by ambition to establish itself as a great imperial power, led off with the eight-shot Mauser rifle in 1884. Afraid to let the Germans get too far ahead, France followed suit the next year. Britain and Austria adopted repeaters in 1886. By 1900 the repeater was universal.

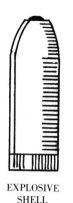

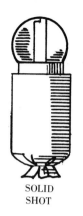

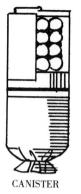

MORTAR
SHELL

EXPLOSIVE
SHELL

SOLID
SHOT

CANISTER

Shot comes

from the Anglo-Saxon *scot* or *sceot*, a form of the verb *sceotan*, meaning "to shoot." This Anglo-Saxon word goes back to an old Germanic root something like *skut*, meaning "to throw, push, or shoot."

In modern usage, *shot* refers to small pellets such as those in a shotgun shell. But the original meaning of *shot* was an arrow shot from a bow or one of the various missiles thrown by catapults and other siege engines. As cannons took the place of siege engines, men began calling cannonballs *shot*. By the late 1400's the term had been stretched to include bullets for shoulder guns as well.

In the armies of Henry VIII of England, in the 1500's, *the shot* meant the bowmen and handgunners, who were organized in separate companies apart from the pikemen, billmen, halberdiers, and swordsmen. As time went on, *the shot* came to consist more and more of gunners and less and less of bowmen. Just before the end of that century, Queen Elizabeth abolished the bow as a military weapon, and *the shot* meant soldiers armed with arquebus or musket. A century later, *the shot* had dropped out of use as a special term, since it now covered practically everybody.

150

As far back as the early 1500's, hunters had used small shot pellets for hunting birds. The pellets spread out in a wide pattern and so were much more likely to hit a target, especially an elusive one like a bird, than a single heavy ball. For larger game, they loaded their smoothbore guns with heavy shot.

At first, heavy shot was made by being cast in molds. Even with molds that cast a number of shot at one time, it was a long process to make enough for a day's hunting. Fine shot was made by cutting a sheet of lead into little squares and rolling them between heavy stone or metal plates until they were more or less rounded off. Shot made this way was never uniform in size and never truly round, so that no two pellets ever behaved the same. Each time you fired your trusty fowling piece, the shot would fly out in a different pattern. This may have made shooting more of a challenge; it certainly decreased the chances of scoring a hit.

Sometime in the 1600's, an impatient sportsman of an inventive turn of mind discovered a faster method of making shot. He poured molten lead through a sieve held over a tub of water. As the lead fell from the sieve in thin streams, surface tension caused it to break up into round droplets. The water cushioned the droplets and instantly cooled and solidified them. The higher the sieve was held, the rounder the droplets were. This made better shot, since the more regular a projectile's shape is, the more regular its flight path is.

In 1782 an English plumber invented the shot tower. This was a tall, slender structure that looked much like a factory chimney. At the top of the tower was a metal plate punched full of holes, through which the molten lead was poured. A plate with large holes was used for making heavy shot, and ones with small holes for fine shot. Since the lead fell for the distance of several stories before it reached the water, it enabled almost perfectly round pellets to form. Usually several sizes of shot were produced at each pouring, as there was always some variation in the size of the lead droplets, but it was easy to sort them out with the aid of a sifter.

Shot for most purposes is still made by the shot-tower method, although today the "tower" is just part of a factory building. But for shooting competitions, such as trap shooting and skeet shooting, the contestants prefer perfectly round shot. This must be produced mechanically.

An old name for shot was *hail shot*, and shot is still known as *hail* in several languages. Later, hunters distinguished between *bird shot*, for small and medium-sized birds, *swan shot*, for large birds, and *buckshot*, for big game such as deer. (*Buck* is a common name for "male deer." For some reason it is also used for a male rabbit. But it is not recommended to shoot a rabbit with buckshot if you want to have anything left for the stewpot.) *Buckshot* once meant the distance from which it was proper to shoot a buck. That was in the 1400's. By the time of the American Revolution it had taken on its present meaning.

Today birdshot ranges in size from .03 inch, with more than 5,000 pellets to the ounce, to .175-inch diameter and 55 pellets to the ounce. This largest size of birdshot also doubles as the familiar BB pellet used in air guns. Buckshot ranges from .25-inch diameter, with about 19 pellets to the ounce, to .36-inch diameter and 7 to the ounce. This is larger in diameter than any modern military bullet, though not as heavy.

Artillerymen formerly made a sharp distinction between *shot* and *shell*. Shot was a solid ball. Shell was a hollow projectile filled with gunpowder which was exploded by a fuse. This is what Tennyson meant when he used the line "stormed at by shot and shell" in his poem *The Charge of the Light Brigade*, which every schoolchild, including this author, once had to memorize.

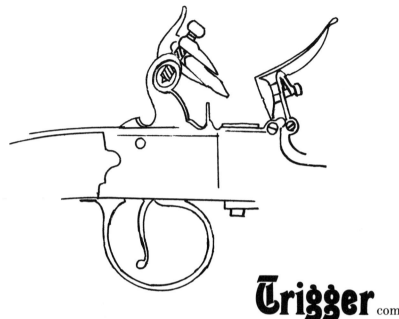

Trigger comes

from the Dutch *trekker*, derived from *trekken*, "to pull." In English, it was originally called a *tricker*, but this form was apparently confused with an older word, *trigger*, which meant a kind of chock or wedge placed under the wheel of a wagon to keep it from rolling. The trigger of a weapon, as most people know, is a small, movable catch that releases the firing mechanism when pressed. *Trigger* was added to the English vocabulary around 1620.

The trigger existed before guns did. Crossbows had a trigger to release the catch that held the bowstring in shooting position. When the matchlock gun was invented, about 1475, a kind of trigger was used to lower the burning match to the priming pan and set the gun off. Since then, triggers have been an indispensable part of all hand and shoulder guns.

A *hair trigger* is a special type of trigger that goes off at a very light touch. This has two advantages. No heavy pull on the trigger is needed; this might cause the gun to move and spoil the shooter's aim. And the light touch decreases the chance of the shooter's flinching, which spoils his aim even more. The hair trigger was invented in Europe about 1700 for use with hunting rifles. German and Swiss immigrants took it to Pennsylvania and made it a feature of the frontiersman's long rifle, later known as the Kentucky rifle.

As a symbol of control, the trigger appears in a few common expressions. A person who is "quick on the trigger" is quick to act or to grasp a meaning. We speak of "triggering" a chain of events—that is, setting them off. A person with a "hair-trigger temper" is likely to explode into rage at the slightest opportunity.

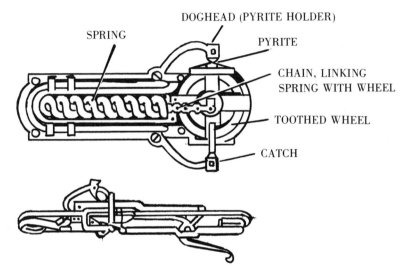

DOGHEAD (PYRITE HOLDER)

SPRING

PYRITE

CHAIN, LINKING
SPRING WITH WHEEL

TOOTHED WHEEL

CATCH

Leonardo da Vinci sketched this design
for a wheel lock in the early 1500's

Wheel Lock was

an early device for firing a gun. It worked on the same principle
as a modern cigarette lighter.

The wheel lock's main working part was a small steel wheel
with a roughened rim. The rim of the wheel extended through a
slot into the priming pan of the gun. While a spring made the

wheel revolve rapidly, a piece of iron pyrite was pressed against the rim, creating a shower of sparks that ignited the powder. The pyrite was clamped firmly in the jaws of a pivoted holder that was called a *doghead*, perhaps because its shape reminded people of a dog with a bone in his mouth.

To operate a wheel lock, you first wound up the wheel with a little wrench or key called a *spanner*, whose name came from a German word meaning "to pull tight." (In Britain, *spanner* is still the name for a wrench.) Then you slid open the pan cover, poured in a little gunpowder, slid the cover back in place, and pulled the doghead down to rest on it. When you pulled the trigger, the pan cover opened automatically, and a spring pressed the doghead and its chunk of pyrite down against the revolving wheel.

The wheel lock seems to have been invented somewhere in the region that stretches from southern Germany to northern Italy. This region was the home of Europe's most skilled clockmakers and mechanics, and it is almost certain that the wheel lock was invented by a clockmaker. Only a clockmaker would have been familiar with the making of little wheels and springs and putting them together so that they would do work.

The oldest references to wheel locks and the oldest examples of that invention come from this region, too. The exact date when the wheel lock was invented is not known, but the oldest known gun equipped with a wheel lock was made between 1521 and 1526, and Leonardo da Vinci sketched out the plans for one before 1517.

The wheel lock was superior to the older matchlock in almost every way. It did not glow to give away its user's position. It could be fired in wind or even rain, both of which would put out a matchlock. A wheel lock could be loaded, primed, wound up, and fired at the user's convenience, hours or even days later, while the matchlock had to be fired within a few minutes of loading.

But the wheel lock was expensive to make, for it had thirty-five or more separate parts, each of which had to be made by hand, one at a time, and painstakingly fitted together. If any of the parts broke, the gun had to be taken to a skilled gunsmith or clockmaker to be repaired. This limited its use to people who could afford an expensive gun and were willing to take care of it, which the average foot soldier definitely was not.

For this reason, the wheel lock remained chiefly a civilian weapon. Its only important military use was on the big pistols used by sixteenth- and seventeenth-century cavalrymen. Instead of the traditional charge with lances or sabers, each trooper had a pair of pistols at the ready as he galloped toward the enemy. As each rank came within range, the cavalry fired off their pistols, caracoled about, and rode back to the rear of the troop. By the time their turn came again—from fifteen to twenty ranks of horses and riders were used—they had their pistols reloaded and ready for more action.

In civilian life, wheel locks were used on all sorts of hunting guns—arquebuses, muskets, and even rifles—as well as on pistols. Since they were rich men's weapons, wheel locks were made with care and often beautifully decorated. Ivory butts were not uncommon, and a man who was really eager to demonstrate his wealth might order his gun to be mounted in silver. All kinds of ingenious gadgets might be added, like the "optional equipment" on a new car. A gunsmith might install an extra doghead in case the regular one went out of commission or perhaps an old-fashioned matchlock to be on the conservative side. Sometimes the lock was modified so that it could be wound by moving the doghead back and forth, thus eliminating the need for that troublesome little spanner, which was so easy to drop and lose.

Wheel-lock pistols were combines with maces, war hammers, and crossbows. There were double-barreled wheel locks and even some with six or seven barrels, like a primitive revolver.

For all the ingenuity lavished on it, the wheel lock could never really compete with simpler and cheaper arms. The invention of the flintlock was the beginning of the end for the wheel lock. By the mid-1600's it was definitely on the way out. The last known wheel-lock guns produced commercially were a pair of pistols made in Paris in 1829. By then they were merely a curiosity.

About the Author

Peter Limburg, a graduate of Yale University, with an MA in U.S. history from Columbia University, has also written *What's in the Names of Fruit*, an earlier *What's-Behind-the-Word Book*.

His fascination with words began as a young boy, and this is one of his continuing interests.

Mr. Limburg, his wife, and their four children make their home in Bedford, New York, where he enjoys gardening, nature study, hiking, and fishing.

About the Artist

The many books illustrated by free-lance artist W. K. Plummer include *Getting to Know the Missouri River*.

A native of Pennsylvania, William Plummer was graduated from the Philadelphia College of Art, where he later taught drawing and illustration.

Mr. Plummer, his wife, and their two children live in a beautiful old farmhouse in the Pennsylvania Dutch country. Mr. Plummer completely renovated the nearby barn to create a spacious, comfortable studio, where he works on his illustrations.